The Entrepreneur's Journey
from Dreaming to Doing

The Entrepreneur's Journey:
from Dreaming to Doing.
Copyright 2005 by Gene Poor and Rodney Heiligmann.
All rights reserved.
Printed in the United States of America by Bookmaster
Cover design: Carley Augustine
Young entrepreneur on cover: Joey Casado
Accounting consultant: Rick Sealscott

Second Edition

Published and distributed by:
The Dallas-Hamilton Center for Entrepreneurship & Innovation
College Of Business Administration
Bowling Green State University
Bowling Green, Ohio 43403

Library of Congress Control Number: 2005902607

Poor, Gene W.   *
        The entrepreneurial journey: from dreaming to doing /
        Gene Poor, Rodney Heiligmann.
        p. cm.
        Includes glossary and bibliographical references.

        1. New Business Enterprises–Management. 2. Small
        Business–Management. 3. Entrepreneurship.

Other books by Gene Poor and Rodney Heiligmann include:
*Animatronics–A Designer's Resource Guide; The Illusion of
Life; It's Your Dream–I'm Just In It; Everything I Know About
VCT So Far–Fits In My Back Pocket.*

To our Dads

Table of Contents

Introduction

Universities have historically done a decent job of preparing students to be good employees. Maybe we should rephrase that. Some departments within universities have done a decent job of preparing students to be good employees. Some departments couldn't care less if students ever got employed. Shame on them! Somehow being able to think–but unemployed–is good.

Luckily, the two of us have always been involved with the former notion. But our point here is that very few universities have done a good job of preparing students to be entrepreneurs–to be business owners, employers, and creative, innovative change agents.

But that's changing across the country in dozens of universities and colleges. And for the life of us–we can't figure out what took them so long to realize the importance of the entrepreneurial spirit.

We recently heard one of the academic gurus of entrepreneur education speak at a seminar. His presentation was exciting and very enjoyable. His description of his entrepreneur program was nothing short of incredible. When we asked him how many of his faculty had ever been entrepreneurs themselves, he replied, "None." His response reminded us of the joke about the definition of a consultant: "They know how to make love 200 ways, but they don't know anybody of the opposite sex."

Well that's not the case here. Both of us are trained academics who have spent our lives simultaneously both in the classroom and in the hot seat of business and industry. Together we bring somewhere in the neighborhood of 50 years of real experience in start-ups and ongoing ventures. So for what it's worth: "We've been there, done it, and even got the t-shirts!" And now we want to accompany you on one of the most exciting journeys life has to offer–becoming an entrepreneur!

Foreword

It's easy to be overwhelmed with starting a new business. Thousands of details are looming over the heads of the entrepreneurs before the doors swing open. Everything can look important and usually does. We have been involved with entrepreneurs in dozens of start-up projects, and one of the most important ideas that we have given those entrepreneurs is a simple "mantra" or formula for getting the crucial things done: **gotta-do's, oughta-do's, and niceta-do's.**

First, we tell them to take a moment and list what needs to be done. Please–we know how painful that task can be. Entrepreneurs simply believe that they don't have time to stop and make a list with so much hanging over their heads. But trust us–we've been there ohhhh so many times. The reality is that everything isn't going to get done, and we want to make sure that the crucially important stuff does.

Now once the list is made, we want the entrepreneur to draw a circle around the crucial "gotta-do items." The tendency is to circle everything. But everything isn't crucial. Many things ought to be done, but the business could open without them. Let's draw a square around those "oughta-do" elements. And what you'll begin seeing is that there are just some "niceta-do" items that we can forget about for a while until we're up, and running and can spend some time on frivolous details.

So with our new prioritized list in hand, we can go back to the work of focusing on the "gotta-do's" and, if time permits, the "oughta-do's." And yes, someday in the future the "niceta-do's." Probably way in the future.

Does the system work? ABSOLUTELY! In fact, we used it in preparing this book. We have identified what we think are the "gotta-do's" of entrepreneurship, and we're only presenting those. (OK–maybe just a few "oughta-do's" and "nicta-do's.")

From dreaming to doing 1.

"If you can dream it, you can do it."
Walt Disney

The traditional definition of an entrepreneur is simply a person who starts, organizes, and operates a business. But over the past few years, the term entrepreneur has taken on a broader definition. It's now defined as a state of mind. It's about having a passion for doing something you love. It's about a spirit. It's about a "can-do" attitude. It's about a unique, opportunity seeking, mind-set.

These "new entrepreneurs" like to do things differently. They like to bend the rules and excite the world with their off-the-wall ideas. New entrepreneurs typically look for unique opportunities in which to direct their passions and energy. The new entrepreneurs are as much about creativity, innovation, ideas, and change as they are about starting a business.

Hence the entrepreneurial spirit can be found in anyone–anywhere. It can be a magician like David Copperfield whose passion for magic has manifested itself into a variety of outlets, including an immense traveling act, a web site, books, magic kits–even an island. It can be found in an entertainer like Oprah Winfrey with her television show, magazine, and empire. It can be a group of university students who start a Dance Marathon to raise money for charity. It can be a university professor who creates a unique academic program. It can be an employee of a large corporation who devises a new system for manufacturing a product. It can be a waiter who develops a unique serving system to better treat customers. It can even be a housekeeper who devises new inventory and shopping techniques that streamline weekly purchases.

This spirit is ultimately a way of improving life. As Guy Kawasaki states in *The Art of the Start*, "The reality is that

"Don't confuse efforts with results."
Thomas Barrack, Jr.

"The highest art form is really business. It is an extremely creative form, and can be more creative than all the things we classically think of as creative. In business, the tools with which you're working are dynamic: capital and people and market and ideas. (These tools) all have lives of their own. So to take those things and to work with them and reorganize them in new and different ways turns out to be a very creative process." (1).
Wayne Van Dyke

"Energy. It's 75% of the job. If you haven't got it, be nice."
Paul Arden

9

the word entrepreneur is not a job title. It is a state of mind of people who want to alter the future."[2]. Kawasaki, who was one of the individuals responsible for the success of the Macintosh computer, goes on to explain that no one really knows if he or she is an entrepreneur until they become one–and sometimes not even then. His test is only one question before starting any new venture, "Do I want to make meaning?"

And according to Kawasaki "meaning" is not about money, power, prestige, or even a fun place to work. But meaning would include making the world a better place to live or increasing the quality of human life. The essence of what Kawasaki says is that "the causation of great organizations is the desire to make meaning. Having that desire doesn't guarantee that you'll succeed, but it does mean that if you fail, at least you failed doing something worthwhile."[3]

No matter which definition of an entrepreneur you prefer, the fundamentals of the journey remain the same–and they all start with dreaming. The danger of the start activity is that most people never move into doing. And doing is the essence of being an entrepreneur. Doing takes you out of being a spectator and puts you into the world of being a participator. And that's where all the action and excitement takes place.

Our assumption is that you have already been dreaming. This book is about doing something! Hopefully, it is something with meaning, but the emphasis is on getting to the doing phase. We will focus on the traditional business start-up journey but with the "new entrepreneur" focus on creativity, innovation, ideas, and change.

Savor the journey!

Coulda, woulda, shoulda's 2.

A lot of books on entrepreneurship begin with a quiz to see if you have the right stuff. But we have no evidence that there is a correlation between the right stuff and success in pursing an entrepreneurial venture. What you say you'll do and what you'll actually do are often two very different things. (We learned that from actual customer behavior.) So instead, we decided to start out by giving you some homespun, entrepreneurial advice. Here are ten ideas to seriously consider:

First, if at all possible–do what you know. Build your ideas around your personal knowledge base, your hobbies, your skill sets, your passions, or your heritage. (You might be a "lucky-spermer.") Otherwise, you probably won't have enough time or money to learn the business before it goes belly up!

Second, we highly recommend working for someone who is doing what you want to do before you start your venture. This way you can learn the unique business specifics from them, see if it's really something you want to do, and, better yet, make your mistakes on their dime and time.

Third, learn and understand the mechanics of business. Technical knowledge is a very small part of the overall business venture. Sales and management skills are far more important in the success of your venture.

Fourth, have an industrial-grade work ethic. Know going in that you will spend more time on this project than most people can begin to muster. Remember, there won't be a lot of therapy and recreational time on your agenda if you decide to pursue this. And you sure won't have much spare time if you "buy-in" to our fifth recommendation.

Fifth, don't quit your day job. Having a separate income removes the desperation involved in starting a business. The

According to a survey by *Global Entepreneurship Monitor* (GEM) only one in 11 people has entrepreneurship instincts. This report was the largest ever measure of entrepreneurial activity worldwide, studying a workforce of 784 million people in 34 countries. (4)

pressure of the business supporting itself will be big enough without laying your personal financial obligations on top of it. Many people won't agree with this notion because they believe that you need to spend all your time on the new venture. But that's where our sixth recommendation becomes crucial.

Sixth, bootstrap your start-up venture. Start your business at a bare-bones level. If at all possible, reduce it to the minimum requirements to beta-test your idea. Keep your costs and risks as low as possible. As the business builds in strength, you can expand as necessary.

Seventh, get a mentor who knows business. Ideally this will be someone who knows your business area. Select this person carefully and you'll trim months off your start-up, reduce your mistakes, and stabilize your sanity level (nothing like a hug).

Eighth, pick your partners carefully. If you're confident that you need them, be sure they have the necessary "chutzpah" that they say they have. Have you seen proof or just heard stories? Remember effort and performance are not the same thing. You're only interested in performance and quality—not how hard your potential partners work. Think results!

Ninth, know (or learn before you start) how to sell. Getting and keeping customers will depend on your ability to sell. Getting financing for your business will depend on your ability to sell. Recruiting and retaining the right team will depend on your ability to sell. It has a lot to do with your personality and perseverance. Have you got it?

Tenth, passion is great, but perseverance is the fuel that will power the potential for business profitability and success. Enough said.

Smoke and mirrors. There is a company in Columbus, Ohio, that started building theatrical smoke machines in the owner's basement in the evenings. It progressively grew in sales, became very profitable, and could have easily justified moving into a real manufacturing facility. But the situation was so convenient and so cost effective that the owner resisted moving out of the basement until the neighbors finally protested to the zoning board. Trust us–that's a good problem.

"As a rule of thumb, if the guy who asks you to pick a card, any card, is wearing a top hat, he's not giving you a real choice."

Penn Jillette

Makin' it 3.

"The basics of a successful business: The product costs a penny; you sell it for a dollar; and everybody wants one."

Anonymous

Business is about making money. As silly as it may seem, a lot of people have a hard time with that basic premise. They believe that profit is a bad word. Nothing could be further from the truth. (We hope you're not one of them but if you are–we'll attempt to alter that notion.) People forget that if businesses didn't make money, they wouldn't have their jobs.

We often hear people say business is too confusing. But business is basically about simple math–adding, subtracting, multiplying, and dividing. Our goal in this section is to make you "financial snapshot road warriors." We want you to routinely look at different businesses with our financial snapshot technique (primarily start-ups) and decide for yourself if they have a chance to survive. You'll notice that financial snapshots generally consider only two of the many expenses involved in a typical business–rent and labor. But these are generally the two most critical and expensive cost factors.

It is imperative that you master the use of financial snapshots. This is an extremely powerful tool that will become the basis of many of your decisions about a business's potential. Trust us–learn this technique, and you'll dazzle your family, friends, and relatives. Let's take a look at how it works.

Margin

Every business offers a range of goods or services for sale. The difference between what it costs to produce those goods/services and what a business can charge for those goods/ services is called margin. Margin is really all a company has to work with to stay alive. For the above quote *"The basics of a*

High as a kite. A kite store recently opened in our community. They had a small store front in the downtown area. Evidently this entrepreneur thought since our town is known for its gusty wind, that his business would be a natural success. The average kite price was about $10.00. His cost was probably $5.00–so his margin was $5.00. We're guessing his rent was about $600.00 a month. Hence, he had to sell 120 kites a month to just pay his rent ($600.00 ÷ $5.00). The owner was the only person working the store, and he kept his hours to a minimum of about 100 a month. Here is an example of an entrepreneur who kept his regular day job and just wanted to see if the market was strong enough to sustain his business. Although he didn't really need to pull labor costs out of the business, sales weren't strong enough to even pay the rent.

13

successful business: the product costs a penny; you sell it for a dollar..." the margin is 99¢ (a penny subtracted from a dollar). The margin is what we want you to focus on as a beginning entrepreneur. Once more–say it out loud: "Margin is the difference between what something costs and what it can be sold for."

Financial snapshots

Select a business–preferably a small local start-up with a simple product. Now guess what their margin might be. Yes, this is where you have to play your hunches. Try to make an educated guess. Be patient–you'll get better at guessing as you learn to use this technique and you develop a "business savvy." Now take another guess at what you think the rent might be for the business. (Better yet, go to a local real estate office and inquire what the rent is for a typical storefront.) Now divide the margin into the rent. This will tell you how many of those products have to be sold to just pay the rent.

$$\text{Rent} \div \text{margin} = \text{number of units}$$

For example, we had a student entrepreneur propose a wall-poster store which would be located in a vacant downtown building. He ran a financial snapshot on his idea. He could buy posters for $4.00 and was going to sell them for $8.00. (Many retail stores work on this 100% mark-up concept.) His margin was $4.00. His rent for the building was $1,000.00 a month. He had to sell 250 posters a month to just pay the rent. That fact alone put fear in his eyes!

$$\$1,000.00 \div \$4.00 = 250 \text{ posters}$$

Now if the first financial snapshot still looks viable, let's take a look at labor cost–the real business killer! Establish how many hours the business is open each day, how many days a month, and how many employees are required for operation. Again

No rent control here! We know a restaurant/bar in New York City that has rent of $60,000 a month and labor of $140,000–for a total of $200,000.00. Their food/liquor product has an average cost of 20¢ on the dollar. Hence their margin is 80¢. Consequently, they have to sell $240,000.00 a month in product just to pay the rent and labor. They can do it in New York City. I doubt if they could do anywhere else in the country. In fact, they tried in Chicago and Dallas and failed miserably. Only the sheer amount of tourists in New York City allows those numbers to work out.

play your hunches. Try to make an educated guess. And then try to figure out what the going wage might be. If it's a simple venture, use $7.00 an hour, roughly what minimum wage actually costs most businesses after they add taxes, unemployment, workers compensation, etc. Multiply all those numbers together to establish a monthly labor cost. Then divide the monthly labor cost by the margin. This will tell you how many of the products have to be sold to just pay the labor costs.

Hours x days x # of employees x wage = labor cost ÷ margin

For the poster store, the entrepreneur was going to be open every day from 9:00 to 9:00 with one person staffing the store and receiving $7.00 an hour (actually two shifts with one person working).

12 x 30 x $7.00 = $2520 ÷ $4.00 = 630 posters

Now if you add the 250 posters it would take to pay the rent to the 630 posters it would take to pay the labor, you get a grand total of 880 posters. Our young entrepreneur looked at that number and went from "What a great idea" to "What was I thinking?" There wasn't a chance in the world he could sell that many posters a month at that particular storefront location.

For practice, let's take a financial snapshot of a service-type business—for instance a barbershop. Barbers in this area of the country are currently charging approximately $11.00 a haircut. Of that $11.00, we should probably allow $1.00 for razor/scissor sharpening and/or replacement. Hence, $11.00 minus $1.00 leaves a $10.00 margin. Let's assume that the rent for a small downtown barbershop would be $800.00 a month. If we divide the $10.00 margin into the rent of $800.00, we find that the barber has to give 80 haircuts a month to just pay the rent. That's 20 haircuts a week or almost 3 per day to just pay the rent. How many haircuts to you suppose the barber must give to pay the other expenses?

Taxi! Taxi drivers in New York City have different options in terms of how they operate. One of the most popular is to lease a cab for a twelve-hour shift. Drivers must pay the cab company $150.00 up front before they leave with the cab, and they also must pay for all gasoline expenses, which generally amount to another $50.00. So until they have collected $200.00 for cab rides–the cab drivers are personally not making any money. Some days they barely make the $200.00. Other times they can make an adequate living working a 12-hour shift. Their margin is anything over $200.00. The margin can be divided by 12 hours to find out their gross hourly wage. For example, let's say that they took in $350.00 in cab fares. Subtract the $200.00 from the $350.00 for a sum of $150.00. Divide the $150.00 by 12 for a total of a $12.50 per hour gross wage.

Got your attention yet? If you are like most student entrepreneurs, you're wondering how does the barber make a living? Let's use our snapshot system to go a little deeper. Let's guess that his/her total miscellaneous expenses are another $1,000.00 a month. Divide the $10.00 margin into that, and we find that the barber must give another 100 haircuts a month to cover those expenses. Now let's say the barber wants to make $36,000 a year (or $3,000 a month). Divide the $10.00 margin into $3,000 and you get 300 haircuts. Now let's add all the haircuts together for a grand total of 480 a month or 120 a week or 20 a day. Can it be done? If they can do 4 haircuts an hour–that's only 5 hours for the 20 haircuts. It can be done if they can get the customers in the door! Ahhh customers in the door–there's a great topic. If more than 20 customers a day come in, the barber is making decent money!

We recently took our company car to a local "start-up" car-detailing business located in a small building near downtown. The owner was charging $50.00 to detail any car. That price included an interior shampoo and exterior waxing. We asked how many cars the owner could do in a day, and he replied two, because he had no other employees. Let's apply the financial snapshot and see if he'll be around in six months. Let's start with rent and guess it to be $500.00 a month. He charges $50.00 a car, but we have to subtract at least $5.00 for supplies. So his margin per car is $45.00. If he works 20 days a month and can somehow do 2 cars a day without ever having a rain day– he can take in $1800.00. Subtract the rent of $500.00 and we're left with $1300.00. Divide his time of 160 hours (4 x 40 hours) into $1300.00, and you find that he is only working for a little over $8.00 an hour. Last person out–please turn off the lights. He did a couple of weeks later.

Let's look at applying the financial snapshot yet another way. We know that a local portrait photographer works out of small studio she rents from a strip mall for $1200.00 a month. She has one employee who makes minimum wage and works 40

A trucker's story. Even truck drivers have margin problems, especially those who try to make it as independent haulers. The problem is simply that they don't know what their actual per-mile costs are before they bid a hauling job. Currently, the average per-mile cost of operating an 18-wheeler is about 90¢ a mile. The drivers need to charge more than 90¢ to create a margin. Many drivers will bid something like 70¢ a mile just to win the job from competing truckers, who also don't know their actual costs. What the drivers fail to understand is basic math. You can't charge less than what it costs to operate the truck–at least for very long. Just consider how fuel-cost changes can affect truckers who often only get 2-3 miles per gallon. Trucking is a tough business with very small margins.

hours a week. She pays herself $1000.00 a week. She charges a flat rate of a $100.00 for her photo services; she also charges for whatever prints the client wants to purchase. We know a good part of her income is from the margin on the photographic print orders. That aside, let's just look at what she needs to do to pay her rent and labor costs. Adding up the studio rent, minimum-wage employee, and her own wage–we're looking at over $6000.00 a month. Dividing her $100.00 portrait flat rate into $6000.00, we find that our photographer must take 60 portraits a month (or 15 a week). That seems like a viable business IF she can generate the customer traffic. In addition, more money can be made because portrait photographers often branch out into wedding photography for weekends.

Let's take a look at a tattoo parlor. We're told that the average college-student tattoo costs between $50 and $100.00. So let's settle on $75.00 as our margin. (We won't even guess at ink and needle cost.) Most of our local tattoo parlors are located in downtown storefronts that rent out for at least $1000.00 a month. Dividing $75 into the rent gives us about 13 tattoos a month to pay the rent. But here's where it gets tough–who really knows what a tattoo artist wants to make as a monthly salary? For the sake of this experience, let's say $3,000 a month or $36,000 a year! Dividing $75 into $3,000 gives us 40 tattoos a month (or 10 a week) to pay their wages. Adding those 10 to the 3 for rent gives us 13 a week. Seems to us that they can do that as long as the tattoo life cycle continues.

Take a stroll down any main street business area and begin performing financial snapshots. Look especially for the new start-up ventures. They're the most volatile. Notice the explosion of new ice cream shops, scrapbook stores, copy centers, health food outlets, specialty coffee shops, cookie/donut stores, cold sandwich shops, tanning booths, piercing and tattoo parlors, and nail salons. Select one and apply the financial snapshot technique and you'll be absolutely

A handle on margin!
I am always amazed at how few people really understand the concept of margin. Even professional business people who live it every day often confuse the basic financial concepts of business. A restaurant owner friend recently wanted to increase his holiday sales by having a simple folding table set-up in the mall to sell gift certificates. The mall charged him $1,000 a week for the table space. I asked him how the technique was going, and he said he paid for the table space the first day by selling ten $100.00 certificates. But he was mistaken– he's confusing cash flow for margin.

17

amazed at what you will discover about their viability and the possibility of their survival.

Does the financial snapshot system always work? Absolutely not. Do any systems? There are too many factors involved to reliably predict a business's success/failure potential.
For instance, established businesses often don't have to pay rent because their buildings are paid for. Some businesses exist simply to provide the owners access to legitimate tax deductions for their interests that they couldn't get if they kept them as hobbies. Some businesses count on the fact that they can use non-pay interns to offset their labor expense. Other businesses are too complicated for us to perform a simple financial snapshot on them. And some organizations incorporate very unique business models that defy determining how they survive and make a profit.

The important part about practicing this technique is that you fully understand the concept of margin and the impact it has on business success. Later in the book, that skill will be very valuable in determining break-even points.

Customers–what's in it for me? **4.**

"If I build it–will they come?" is the premise for <u>Field of Dreams</u>, *a very successful film that grossed over 65 million dollars at the box office.*

"When I open the doors–the customers will come" is said thousands of times a year by hopeful entrepreneurs only to be badly mistaken. These people eventually will lose millions of dollars in the process.

Customers buy for only three reasons: to feel good, solve a problem, or both. Going out to a movie, buying a model airplane, or getting a new kitten are all part of the "feel good" notion. Buying a mousetrap, getting an oil change, or having the lawn mowed professionally are all part of the "solve a problem" category. Going to a fancy restaurant, buying a sports car, and getting a big-screen television incorporates both reasons.

Customers don't buy products and services: They buy what they get from the products and services. For instance, they don't buy medicine–they buy cures. They don't buy gasoline–they buy transportation. They don't buy flowers– they buy hope. They don't buy a college degree–they buy a better education and lifestyle. They don't buy drills–they buy holes. They don't buy an oil change–they buy a longer-running engine.

In his book *How to Make Big Money in Your Own Small Business*, Jeffrey Fox list the three most important rules to the success of any business:
1. Having a customer
2. Getting a customer
3. Keeping a customer.

Fox explains that rule #1–Having a customer–is more

We believe that people say the same four things to themselves a thousand times a day: Who cares? So what! What's in it for me? And this better be good!

To the entrepreneur, the customer is king and queen.

"What does it take to find a stranger, reach that stranger, teach that stranger, and then get that stranger to walk into a store and buy what you're selling? It's too hard."

Seth Godin

19

important than the business idea, opportunity, management, location, or anything else. This simply means that there is someone on the planet who would pay for your product or service. Getting that person to buy is second in importance, and keeping that person buying is third.[5]

The **first question** every potential entrepreneur should ask is why should the customer do business with me? The **second question** is why should the customer do business with me and not the competition? The answer must be a benefit to the customer—*a value proposition*! And the answer always incorporates the customer's agenda, attitude, and value system. (The customer's value and attitudes are part of what marketers refer to as an individual's psychographics.)

The **third question** every entrepreneur should ask is who is the customer? Marketing researchers refer to this as creating a customer profile. Some of the customer demographic attributes include:
1. Customer base–Is it widespread or a niche?
2. Geographic–Are the customers' buying needs and preferences unique to the location?
3. Gender–Each has unique buying habits.
4. Age–Amounts of disposable income vary by age.
5. Disposable income–Money doesn't always determine how people will spend it or on what.
6. Education–Often determines what media people experience, which can help entrepreneurs select advertising mediums.

The **fourth question** every entrepreneur should ask is how do I get the customer to come to my business? The answer to that question is selling! Selling will become the most important activity your business will do. There's an old but golden saying in business, "Nothing happens until a sale is made." That concept is so important, it has its own chapter. More later!

"If you don't select a niche market for your business, you don't have a chance for survival."
Donald Trump

". . . put one niche in your basket, hatch it, put another niche in your basket, hatch it . . . and soon you'll have a whole bunch of niches that add up to market domination."
Guy Kawasaki

20

Creativity and innovation 5.

We're sure that ideas are the lifeblood of an entrepreneur. And we're also sure that creative ability is the quality of the individual who generates those ideas. But what is the process a creative person uses to generate and implement new ideas?

Roger von Oech describes such a process in his book *A Kick in the Seat of the Pants*. Roger believes that creative people go through four distinct stages as they develop ideas:

Stage 1–The **explorer** is looking for opportunity, pain, difficulty, weirdness, spin-offs, problems–anything that causes a stir within your soul.

Stage 2–The **artist** turns resources into new ideas and solutions.

Stage 3–The **judge** evaluates ideas to see if they have potential.

Stage 4–The **warrior** carries the best idea into the world with the passion of an evangelist.(6)

During his first year of teaching high school, Gene Poor watched the football coach progress through those four stages of creative development. His name was Harry Gilcrest, and he loved coaching but hated the process of removing the bandages from the players' knees and elbows after practice each night. He recognized that problem as an **explorer**. As an **artist,** he searched for solutions and came up with dozens of different devices that used razor blades, knives, and scissors. As a **judge**, he evaluated each one of his potential solutions (actually on his players) and eventually decided on one that was a spin-off of his wife's seam ripper from her sewing basket. It had the same shape handle but included a single-sided razor blade. As a **warrior**, Harry had to fabricate the cutter and then get it into the marketplace by working with various manufacturers and sport distributors across the country. Over the years, Harry has sold thousands of Gilcrest cutters to every sports team in the world. If you've played on a team and had bandages put on,

"Truly ground-breaking ideas are rare, but you don't necessarily need one to make a career out of creativity. My definition of creativity is the logical combination of two or more existing elements that result in a new concept. The best way to make a living with your imagination is to develop innovative applications, not imagine completely new concepts."

Sam Weston
Creator, GI Joe figure

"All human development, no matter what form it takes, must be outside the rules; otherwise, we would never have anything new."

Charles Kettering

"Creativity is thinking up new things. Innovation is doing new things."

Theodore Levitt

you've probably removed them with a *Gilcrest Cutter*. Harry's famous line describing the experience was, "I paid off my home's mortgage and put two kids through medical school with that silly product. Oh yeah, and I bought myself a new Mercedes every year."

Charles Thompson, in his book *What a Great Idea!*(7), believes that ideas come from "Ready, Fire . . . Aim! Thinking." He explains that the steps are:
1. *Define your problem (Ready).*
2. *Come up with as many ideas as you can as fast you can without criticizing them (Fire).*
3. *Sift, synthesize, and choose (Aim).*

Thompson's approach uses a time-tested concept of generating large quantities of ideas through "brainstorming" as a fundamental part of his process. Instead of thinking internally about a problem, the thinker or group looks elsewhere for solutions: up, down, in, out, forward, backward, upside down, inside out. It's all based on Thompson's first Creative Rule of Thumb: "The best way to get great ideas is to get lots of ideas and throw the bad ones out."

Some of Thompson's other Rules include:
- *Create ideas that are fifteen minutes ahead of their time . . . not light years ahead.*
- *Always look for the second right answer.*
- *If at first you don't succeed. . . take a break.*

While creativity is the ability to bring an idea into existence, innovation is the process of refining that idea into a tangible product or service. As Peter Drucker (the management guru) states, "Business has only two functions, marketing and innovation."(8) (And you'll notice that both of those functions rely heavily on the creative process as a common denominator.) It is simply those entrepreneurial companies that can quickly develop and implement innovative products and services that

"When you ask a dumb question, you get a smart answer."
Aristotle

"No matter what you are currently able to do, creativity can make you capable of doing more."
John Maxwell

"Look at more stuff, and think about it harder."
Andy Sefanovich

"The hero is the one with the ideas."
Jack Welch

will be successful in the future. The primary question that the entrepreneur must continually ask is, "How can we be different and/or unique?"

Most creative "how-to" books describe various techniques on generating new ideas on how to think differently. These include:

- **Mind mapping** which involves writing a stimulus word in the center of a piece of paper and then quickly writing down as many words as you can that are associated with that word. The idea is to look for new relationships and associations.
- **Metaphors** are ways of making complex ideas easier to understand. We heard an executive describe his conservative company by saying, "It's like a living organism in that it would kill any new, strange idea– much the way a human body fights off infection."

- **What if** is a technique of looking at things and asking contrary and nonexisting questions. For instance, what if everyone had to own a "side business" to survive? Would that make them better employees? Would that make them better customers?
- **Break the rules** is a way of looking at things by removing the assumed rules. This is a technique you can use on things, processes, and even yourself. Would you be willing to not take lunch and two breaks if you could leave 90 minutes earlier from work each day?

- **Change vantage points** is a way of looking at a problem from a different perspective. Think about how a customer views your product or process. For instance, if you were the customer how would you feel about being sent to voice mail every time you called?
- **Think backwards** is doing the opposite of what you normally would do. Instead of reading about how to interview for a job–read how to give an interview. It will give you insight in how an interviewer thinks.

See chapter 51 for additional thoughts on generating ideas.

6. Sources of business ideas

Although some people just naturally seem to have an unlimited supply of ideas for businesses, others seem to need a creative nudge. Here are some sources for inspiration:

1. What are you the king or queen of? What do you really do well? That inherent skill could be the basis for a booming business. (This is how a neatness freak started a space-organizing company.)
2. How about converting a hobby into a business (e.g., quilting, comics, trading cards, scrapbooks)?
3. If you are currently employed, is that company ignoring something that needs to be done in the marketplace that you could do?
4. If you are a student, is there something that needs to be done on campus that you could develop? (That's precisely how Kinkos got started.)
5. Look for problems or pain that are not being solved by any company in the area. (That's how a speedy delivery service was created.)
6. Consider buying a franchise. Many magazines and web sites list and describe the hot ones on the move.
7. Look at an existing business and determine if you could do it differently.
8. Bring a business that you've seen elsewhere to your neighborhood and put your unique twist on it.
9. Read the yellow pages. Seriously–this is a great source of inspiration. You will be dazzled by the variety of businesses that you never knew existed.
10. Watch the Discovery Channel and HGTV for new trends and ideas that could develop into a business.
11. Read magazines from disciplines you wouldn't normally experience–think backwards.
12. Look within your family for spin-off opportunities/ interests that other members may possess.

"Make it a practice to keep on the lookout for novel and interesting ideas that others have used successfully. Your idea only has to be original in its adaptation to the problem you are working on."
Tom Edison

"All art is theft."
Picasso

"The originality of your idea is based on the obscurity of your design source."
Anonymous

"Nothing is new except arrangement."
Will Durant

"Originality is the art of concealing your source."
Tom Edison

Idea vs. business opportunity 7.

An important distinction you need to make is that an idea and a business opportunity are not necessarily the same. You can generate literally hundreds of ideas. But only a few have the potential of being a business opportunity. A business opportunity is an idea with commercial viability that can generate money and in some way create value for a customer.

In the book *Entrepreneur's Toolkit*(9), a series of questions were presented as business opportunity checkpoints:

1. Does it create value for the customers in such a way that they may have to pay a premium price?
2. Can the business profitably deliver the product or service?
3. Is the potential profit in alignment with the potential business risk?
4. Is there adequate expertise among the founder and management team?
5. Does the idea have a significant life duration to exploit the business?
6. Is the idea fundable?

Of all of the above checkpoints, the first one is often the most difficult to understand. Customers will pay for a product or service only if they perceive a benefit whose value is greater than its price. Remember, in the business world they refer to this as *value proposition*. In other words, why will the customer buy from you? Always keep in mind the customer mantra: "What's in it for me?"

Ultimately, to be successful in the market place, a business opportunity will need to evolve into an entrepreneur's business model. A business model is basically an entrepreneur's plan of how their business will create customer value, maintain momentum, and simultaneously make a profit.

"Great ideas, like humor, come from the corners of the mind, out on the edge. That's why humor can break up log-jams in both personal relationships and in business."
Kevin Roberts

"I want to stay as close to the edge as I can without going over. Out on the edge you see all kinds of things you can't see from the center."
Kurt Vonnegut

8. Niche markets

T-shirts. When Rick Kramer started his silk-screening business a number of years ago, he needed a "niche" to differentiate himself from a half dozen other t-shirt companies in the area. He creatively came up with the concept of printing hospital names on t-shirts for infants: "Born here in Wood County Hospital." His idea took off, and he was very successful at promoting the idea across the country.

Pin-ball Doctor. When Dr. Scott opened his pin-ball machine store, he had a number of competitors in the area. His "niche" was that he serviced what he sold–something none of the other stores were doing. That's where the title "Dr." comes in. Dr. Scott is a pin-ball machine doctor. Used pin-ball machines are notorious for breaking down, and few people really know how to repair them. He markets his niche with the name Dr. Scott–the Pin-Ball Doctor. It works great!

Tom Dowd sells central vacuums for residential use. He has a lot of competition from a variety of businesses that also sell burglar alarms, sound systems, and whole-house wiring. But Tom concentrates his marketing efforts on people who would build custom homes over $350,000, or basically people who would be more apt to spend the money on a feature that isn't really a necessity. The difference is that his competition markets to the world with moderate sales. Tom concentrates on a niche market and has 10 installation teams to prove his success at moving central vacuums.

Niche marketing speaks to a target audience. Concentrating on a niche market brings you a number of benefits, including more customers, qualified buyers, repeat business, and better word-of-mouth sales. And the simple reason is that you are generally filling an immediate customer need.

In addition, a niche market enables you to focus your sales message with greater accuracy. The more narrowly you define your niche, the easier it is to communicate with the interests of the people in that market. A small niche can also insulate you from the competition. A large company won't bother with it because the sales numbers aren't there, and small companies might simply overlook it–at least until you control it by being the first in the market with your niche.

Kim Gordon[10] has several rules to keep in mind when taking on a new niche:

1. **Meet the customer's unique needs.** The benefits you promise must have special appeal to the market niche. What can you provide that's new and compelling?
2. **Say the right thing.** It is imperative that you speak the customer's language as a person who knows the market from the inside perspective.

3. Always test your market. Check out the competition's position and determine how you will compete against them. If there is no competition, that isn't always good. It is possible that others have tried and failed to penetrate the niche. Move slowly and "beta-test" the market to reduce your risks.

It is crucial for a new venture to identify and estimate the size of the niche market in order to determine if sales are large enough to support the business idea. There must be enough target buyers on a frequent enough basis to sustain your year-to-year company sales, expenditures, and profits. In other words, a thumbtack store or a scotch tape outlet are probably not viable niche ideas. But the following are a couple of niches that were large enough to make serious profits.

Swanson's hardware in Vineland, New Jersey, has been around for over fifty years. They have seen many competitors come and go, including the really big guns. But they have survived because of their niche–*free, fast delivery*. And that's *free, fast delivery* on any item from a lawn tractor to a handful of bolts–generally within 30 minutes. Great niche!

"Jungle" Jim Bonaminio is the owner, fearless leader and creative spark plug behind one of the largest and unique grocery stores: Jungle Jim's International Market in Hamilton, Ohio. This notoriously creative entrepreneur built his market from a tiny roadside produce stand into a four-acre food lovers' paradise. Jim's flamboyant management style is tempered by his uncanny common-sense approach to problem solving. This marketing maverick sports a healthy disregard for the status-quo and applies his personal brand of guerrilla tactics to every aspect of his booming successful business. His niche– "Making grocery shopping fun." (11)

"Don't try to make money doing the things other people can do."
Guy Kawasaki

Bulb problems. I recently had a client who needed Christmas lights that twinkled–not blink. He bought all his regular supplier had, and he needed tons more. He went to the internet and found a site called Bulb. com. They had hundreds in stock. Talk about a great niche market. They didn't try to tackle the whole lighting industry-just the bulbs.

Dent man! When Dave Moore started his dent removal company he needed a niche, so he marketed himself as an expert in the field of dent removal by teaching others the process while he continued practicing the craft. He charged for both the schooling and the tools, while the students worked for free as interns. His teaching expertise was recognized by the high-end car dealers in town which allowed him to charge premium prices for his service.

9. Value

I have always maintained that there really isn't any reality in the world of business, only perception. And nowhere in business does this phenomena play out more than in the discussion, application, and perception of customer values.

Value–that's a word you're going to hear used a lot if you're really thinking about being an entrepreneur. A formal search for the definition of the word "value" would turn up something like *a principle, standard, or quality considered inherently worthwhile or desirable.* Values are what motivate and fulfill you. They fill your work and life with meaning. They simply represent what's important to you. They guide you through your purchasing choices.

Operationalizing "value" for an entrepreneur would give us this definition: *The difference between a customers' anticipated price and the marked price.* If the customers' anticipated price is higher than the actual price, they perceive it a good value. If the customers' anticipated price is lower than the actual price, they consider it a poor value.

To complicate matters, Watts Wacker and Jim Taylor state in their book, *The Visionary's Handbook,* that every product/service has a spot price–a price a customer is willing to pay to achieve ownership. But that spot price changes according to the customer's experience and present circumstances. What's more, those changes cannot be measured across the market segment because concepts of value have become embedded in individual value codes that have an unshared reality–no two people are alike.[12]

The entrepreneurial challenge is to control the anticipated price–the customer's perception of value. And an entrepreneur can do that through elements like a product/service's reputation, workmanship, materials, engineering, design, sales environment, service, safety, and similar kinds of qualities.

Spot pricing.
Coca-cola has kicked around the concept of spot pricing in their vending machines. The machines would have sensors that could detect the temperature and price accordingly. For instance, on a really hot day they would charge a premium price. But on a cold day the price would be much lower. The machine could also detect various flavor inventories and price accordingly for that aspect as well. If there were only three cans of Diet Coke available, but 10 of regular Coke–the Diet Coke would be priced higher.

Features and benefits 10.

Entrepreneurs often like to talk about and advertise their product's or service's features. Features sound good and make good ad copy, but they don't generally mean much to the customer.

Customers have only one thing on their mind–themselves–or "what's in for me!" Consequently your business can only offer three things: make them feel better, solve a problem, or both. In doing those, your product or service has features that have the ability to translate into customer benefits. A feature is something that performs a function. A benefit is something positive that the customer gets from the feature.

If you were selling an automobile you might say that "ABS" is a feature that is standard equipment on your model. If the customer were to ask, "What is ABS?" You would say, "That is our sophisticated automatic braking system!" But the customer probably still does not know what benefit he or she gets from that feature such as better control of braking on wet or ice-covered surfaces.

Roy Williams in his book *The Wizard of Ads*(13) describes a simple technique that some successful sales people use to clear up that lack of understanding associated with the feature/benefit presentation. Williams suggests that after each description of a product or services feature statement, the sales person adds "which means" and then includes the customer's actual meaningful benefit.

For instance, if we were selling you on an animatronic character with the feature of "analog compliant feedback," we would add, "which means that the animated character has faster, smoother movements that your audience would subconsciously process as having a more believable, human look."

11. Differentiation

The secret to effective customer selling is what advertising and marketing professionals refer to as differentiation or **unique selling proposition (USP)**. It is imperative that you can pinpoint what makes your business unique in a world of "me too" competitors. If you can't describe your unique selling proposition, you won't be able to target your sales efforts toward a particular customer market.

Establishing a USP isn't always easy. It requires some serious analysis of what your business is really about. A good way to start is to analyze how other businesses use differentiation in their marketing programs: BMW–The Ultimate Driving Machine; Jaguar–A Different Breed Of Cat; UPS–Moving At The Speed Of Business; Prius–So Advanced It Makes The Future Look Obsolete; Panasonic–Ideas For Life; Lifeformations–So Realistic, We Fool Mother Nature.

If it's done right, good differentiation is inspiring, energizing, and just makes you feel good about a product or service. According to Kawasaki, there are a number of differentiation qualities to aspire to:

1. **Be positive.** Don't bash the competition. Customers only want to know what you can do for them.
2. **Be customer-centric.** Tell what you are–not what you want to become. Stay away from nothing words like *best, leader, safest, biggest, and similar.*
3. **Be empowering.** Be sure everyone who works for you knows your unique selling proposition.[14]

Remember that successful entrepreneurship is not necessarily about having a unique product or service. It is about making your product or service stand out from the market filled with "me too" competition. That is your main objective. Good luck!

Positioning points 12.

Most people doing research in electric-powered automobiles have a sign hanging somewhere in their laboratory that says: "Fast, cheap and far–pick two." You can go fast and far, but not cheap. You can go fast and cheap, but not far. And you can go far and cheap, but not fast. That's the way it has been for as long as the research in electric-powered cars has been going on and will continue until a major breakthrough in technology takes place.

Business has a similar axiom: "Quality, price, or service–pick two." Those three characteristics are positioning points. When entrepreneurs go into business, they generally align themselves with one or two of the three positioning points. Some businesses will try to pick all three but they won't last long. The basic laws of economics will throw them into a financial nosedive.

Pretend for a moment that you want to start a pizza parlor that prepares the product with only natural ingredients (your differentiation). How will you position yourself against the competition? Are you going to offer a better product–which would be quality? Are you going to offer free 15-minute guaranteed delivery–which would be service? Or are you going to offer a less expensive product–which would be price? Now you could offer two of those three characteristics–and many businesses do–but never three, at least not for very long.

There is a tendency for business neophytes to select price as their positioning point. They are known as bottom-feeders. Not a particularly flattering name is it? If they survive for any length of time, it is not unusual for someone else to come along and make the product even cheaper. This is not where you want to go with your business opportunity. Been there–not fun!

"If you want clean, fresh oats, you have to pay a fair price. If you want oats that have been through the horse, they come a little cheaper."
Anonymous

Brake jobs. There were two auto repair service centers across the street from each. One had a sign hanging outside that said: Brake Jobs $25.00. The other one had a sign hanging outside that said: We Fix $25.00 Brake Jobs.

Auto positioning. Automobile manufactures always position their products. The idea is to have a car for every demographic. Consider Chevrolet and their model lineup. The Aveo is positioned to under-35 year olds with incomes between 35-50k. The Impala is positioned to 50-55 year olds with income in the 55-60k range. The Corvette is positioned to 35-55 year olds with income around 135k. Chevrolet's even scrambling to get a "green car" for the ecology minded person.

31

13. What business are you really in?

If you ask movie theater owners, "what business are you in?" You might be surprised at the answer. They would quickly tell you–concessions! The movie gets the customer into the theater, but the profit is really in the soft drinks, popcorn, and candy.

If you were to ask Honda employees, "What business are you in?" You might expect automobiles or motorcycles as the answer, but they would say engines! If you look at their product line the common denominator is engines for anything that might require them, including boats, generators, lawn mowers, snow blowers, compressors, and even airplanes.

If you were to ask people at car rental agencies, "What business are you in?" You might be surprised to hear them reply, "Resale." They make the majority of their profits in selling their cars after they've been used for rentals. Car rental agencies buy at significantly lower fleet prices; hence, they can sell the cars at the end of their rental use with big margins.

Ask Coastal Pets, "What business are you in?" By the name you might think their answer would be something to do with pets. Yes, they started that way by manufacturing leather leashes and collars for animals. But soon they realized that people also wear leather collars, especially Harley Davidson riders. They now have a division just focusing on the "Hog" collars and accessory account that has far better margins than the original pet business.

Be careful as you research and analyze your business and industry. There are direct and indirect competitors, as well direct and indirect opportunities for new customers. The more you can learn about a particular industry's "bandwidth of sales," the better you can position and differentiate yourself in the marketplace.

Market research 14.

Okay, so you have a great idea for a product or service business–something that will have customers flocking through your door. Your gut says," Jump in!" You have to "strike while the iron is hot." Snooze and you'll lose!

But wait just one second. Shouldn't you really determine whether there is a market for your product or service before investing all that time, money, and energy? Are you really in that much of a hurry to look down the barrel of a business disaster? Even the greatest inventor of all time, Thomas Edison, learned the hard way to do market research after a few of his inventions went south. Consider one of his most famous quotes, "I find out what the world needs. Then I go ahead and try to invent it."

Market research is a way of collecting data and information you can use to solve or avoid marketing problems. The goal of market research is to provide you with information about three critical areas: the industry, the consumer, and the competition.

The industry: Examine where it is in its life cycle. Is it expanding or declining? Look for trends and technological changes. Beware of paradigm shifts–when a new technology completely eliminates an existing technology. We're always amazed when we hear people still talking about opening a video rental store. They are simply are out of touch with what is going on in that industry.

The consumer: You want to establish some reasonable product/service sales projections for your specific population through some form of market survey. This is where demographic profiles of the community should be created and evaluated. The most important consumer analysis should focus on how much of a particular sales volume can you expect to take away from competition. You won't typically generate new

33

business volume, but you will simply take it away from existing businesses. We recently asked a local hardware store owner if his business was hurt when Home Depot came to town. His reply was, "Absolutely. There is only so much hardware business in town, and they just carved their share out of the pie."

Know the competition: You will want to know your competition inside and out! Start by examining the sheer number of competitors, locally as well as nationally. (Even if you're not competing with them, it will give you insight into the overall industry.) Study their products/services, marketing/ sales strategies, and production/management techniques. This analysis should eventually provide a snapshot of their strengths/ weaknesses as well as their threats/opportunities. When a local group considered opening a restaurant, they ate lunch and dinner every day for a month at the competition. While they ate very slowly, they counted customers, evaluated the food/portions, and calculated what a typical lunch and dinner patron spent. They knew their enemy! They knew their strengths and their weaknesses.

There are basically two kinds of market research: primary and secondary. Primary research comes directly from the source and secondary research comes from analyzing data that others have collected in their primary research efforts.

Primary research uses a number of basic techniques to gather information, including surveys, focus groups, personal interviews, observation, field trials, response cards, and web feedback. The type of data you need, how much time you have, and the amount of money you're willing to spend will determine which of the techniques you choose for your business.

The vast amount of research most entrepreneurs conduct will be secondary. The best places to start will undoubtedly be your local library and the internet. There will be at least one trade magazine for every product and service business imaginable. They just won't be available at your local magazine store. These specialty magazines are generally connected to specific trade associations for those particular industries. It is paramount that you find the appropriate associations connected with your business because they will be an incredible source for market statistics, trends, new technologies, lists of members, books, and reference materials. If at all possible, attend their national annual trade shows and conferences. Find those specific associations in the *Encyclopedia of Associations,* which is located in most libraries. (It is on the internet but not for free.)

Governmental agencies are also a valuable source for free secondary research information. County agencies are a potential source for population density and distribution figures. The Department of Commerce (www.commerce.gov) has an electronic small business advisor available with links to all the services the government has to offer the business community. The Census Bureau (www.census.gov) will also give you information about what businesses are located in specific counties.

Colleges and universities also are a valuable source for information and assistance. Both undergraduate and graduate students are typically eager to work on "real" data-gathering research projects, and professors are generally available as consultants on all aspects of business development.

Local community organizations, the Chamber of Commerce, and Economic Development Groups offer a vast amount of assistance and information. Some even offer seminars.

15. Feasibility study

This is a very important check point. You need to perform market research on your business idea before continuing any further. Some entrepreneurs refer to this research analysis as a *feasibility study*. Your goal here is to simply discover if your idea has substantial potential as a business opportunity. In other words–does your business model make sense? Simply stated–can it make money?

When you have finished with your market research, you should have an indication of either "yes" or "no" for taking your business idea into the next stage–a full-blown business plan.

As described previously, you need to seek as much information as possible about three critical areas: the industry, the consumer, and the competition. You will also need to perform a quick financial snapshot of your product or service venture. Consider the following questions when performing your research and analysis:

Demographics at work. Wal-Mart knows that their average shopper makes $40,000 a year. Target knows that their average shopper makes $60,000 a year. What do you suppose the average shopper at Tiffany's makes a year?

The Industry:
- What's the business idea?
- Is the idea a business opportunity?
- Does your idea fill a customer's need, or do you have to create one?
- What's the niche your business will serve?
- How unique is your business niche?
- How will you position your business?
- How will you differentiate your business from the competition?
- Where is your idea in its particular life cycle?
- What industry is your business idea a part of?
- What trade associations represent your industry?
- How has that industry been performing overall?
- How has your business idea been performing?
- What are the trends of that industry indicating?

- What's been the success rate of similar ventures in your industry?
- Are there any paradigm shifts on the horizon that could affect your business idea?

The Customer:
- Describe the specific demographics of your customer.
- Describe the customer's psychographics.
- Describe the geographic area of your customer base.
- How many people are you going to target.
- What quantity do you believe you can actually reach in your geographic area (number or percentage)?
- What advertising and marketing techniques do your customers typically experience?
- How do you intend to reach them?
- Where do they usually buy products or services similar to yours?
- What do they usually pay–more, less, or the same?
- What trends do your customers appear to be influenced by?
- Why would your target customer select your business over the other direct and indirect competitors?
- How "fickle" is your customer base?
- What are their buying habits?

The Competition:
- Who are the leading direct competitors in your geographic area?
- Who are the leading indirect competitors in your geographic area?
- How many direct and indirect competitors are there?
- What are their strengths?
- What are their weaknesses?
- How do they position themselves?
- How do they attract customers?
- How many competitors have failed at what you are proposing?

- What did they do wrong?
- What will you do different?
- Is anybody doing what you want to do in another geographic area?
- What would keep them from moving into your area?
- What would you do if they did come into your geographic area and provided that product/service?

Financial Snapshot
- Establish what you think your product or service margin will be.
- Establish what you think your rent might be for the business.
- Now divide the margin into the rent. This will tell you how many of those products or services have to be sold to just pay the rent.
- Establish what you think your labor cost will be for a month.
- Now divide the margin into the labor cost. This will tell you how many of those products or services have to be sold to just pay the labor costs.
- If you're really ambitious, estimate what your other costs might be and divide your margin into those costs.

Analysis and evaluation of the data 16.

Once you gather the data from your market research, you obviously have to analyze and evaluate it. To ultimately get to a "yes" or "no," we are firm believers in shared thinking–that two heads (or more) are better than one. The trick is to get the right people to participate by asking "who are the seasoned professionals that can help me with this?" As John Maxwell describes in his book, *Thinking for a Change,* "To get anything of value out of shared thinking, you need to have people around the table who bring something *to* the table." Maxwell goes on to list some criteria for the selection process, including:

- People whose greatest desire is the success of the idea.
- People who can add value to another's thought.
- People who possess maturity, experience, and success in the issue under discussion.(15)

In Jack Canfield's book, *The Success Principles*, he describes a similar process called "masterminding" where a group of five or six people get together regularly for the purpose of brainstorming, networking, analysis, evaluation, and problem solving. Canfield's key advice in assembling your group would be to select people who are already where you'd like to be in your life. In other words, select successful, bright business people.(16)

Our first advisory group for a start-up restaurant project was made up of an accountant, a lawyer, a banker, a restaurant owner, and a business academic. The insight and unique perspectives they gave us were absolutely incredible. We are sure that we saved a year of false starts by utilizing the power of group think. The networking alone justified the experience!

Did we incorporate everything we learned? Absolutely not. But it did alleviate analysis paralysis–personally fretting over the information to the point that no real decision was ever made.

More Gilcrest. The Gilcrest Cutter story (told earlier in the creativity chapter) was a good example of misinterpreted market research. The research was actually performed professionally and their results showed that the market was simply not large enough to support the manufacturing and distribution of the cutter. What the research firm did not take in consideration was the fact that the cutters would either be stolen or lost during the sport season and that new ones would have to be purchased each year. Gilcrest knew from his own coaching experience that theft and loss would be key factors in his products success. So he marched forward with incredible success.

17. Mentors, heroes, experts, and advisors

The great thing about your business dream is that someone has probably already done it. Why not tap them for information?

Mentor–a wise and trusted counselor. Get a mentor–better yet have a number of mentors. Use these people to help you develop your business dream and to get where you want to go. The right ones will change your life like no other influence. For sure have a mentor who does for a living what you want to do or at least a close profession. Don't add people who can't contribute. Take them to lunch–sometimes they even buy.

> "If you wish to become affluent, associate with economically produc-tive people."
> Thomas J. Stanley

Advice for finding mentors:
1. Start off slowly.
2. Know what you want.
3. Find the right way to ask.
4. Humility is paramount.
5. Show respect.
6. Let them know you are committed to a goal.
7. Show them you know how to work.
8. Let them know you can perform.
9. Know and understand what a pain a follower (like you) can be.
10. Give something back–even if it's a commitment to being a mentor someday.

A good source for a mentor is a group of retired executives who call themselves SCORE (Service Corps Of Retired Executives). They are volunteers, and their services are free. To find a local chapter, contact them at (800) 634 0245 or visit them at www.score.org. They also offer a free email counseling service for quick questions with a 48-hour answer turnaround.

Hero–a person noted for high achievement. Everyone needs a hero. Heroes are role models. They can be alive or dead.

Famous or not famous. Real or even fictional. They lived your dream. They've been there and did it! Study them. Learn from them. See their strengths and their weaknesses. One of the great things about studying your heroes is that you learn that they are human. They have flaws. But in spite of their flaws they lived your dream. What can you learn from their journey? Can you replicate it? Should you replicate it?

Advice about learning from your heroes:
> Read books about them.
> Listen to tapes about them.
> Watch videos about them.
> Make it a goal to meet them.
> If not that–how about a phone call?

Expert–a person with a high degree of skill or knowledge. Sometimes you need help on something that doesn't require a mentor or a hero. An expert might be just what you need. An expert is a shortcut to success. Experts come in all sorts of packages, including seminars, workshops, videos, audio tapes, CD's, books, and the list goes on. Sometimes you learn by following their advice. Sometimes you learn by not following their advice.

Advisory board or team–a group of experienced people to help guide you in your major business decisions. Unlike a Board of Directors, this group has no fiduciary responsibilities to the shareholders or investors. An advisory team should be comprised of mentors, heroes, and experts– people who have the expertise to help identify key issues and assist in major decisions. We know a local entrepreneur who recently formed her advisory team that she referred to as her dream team. It was comprised of her accountant, lawyer, bank- er, brother, and best friend. Some of the critical issues that they helped her with included a succession plan, expansion param- eters, and new product-development directions. We loved her reaction to a recent dream team meeting: "Help like that would cost me thousands of dollars and take years to acquire."

18. Strategy and tactics

Strategy and tactics are both derived from ancient Greek military words. To the Greeks, *strategos* meant "The art of setting up forces before the battle. *Taktikos* referred to "Moving forces in battle." As Stephen Heiman and Diane Sanchez point out in their book, *The New Strategic Selling*, "Strategy must proceed tactics." The authors point out that "Before you can fight at Gettysburg, you've got to get to Pennsylvania." Just as that principle is true for the military, it also true for overall sales, marketing, and business planning.[17]

In his book, *Strategy Plain and Simple,* Michel Robert makes a clear distinction between strategic thinking and strategic planning. Strategic thinking systems determine *what* an organization should look like in the future, and strategic planning systems determine *how* to get there. It is Robert's notion that an entrepreneur should have a serious strategic thinking system in place in order to prosper and outpace the competitors. Entrepreneurs will need to "out-think" their competitors strategically, not "out-muscle" them operationally.[18]

Strategic thinking is a fresh approach to the concept of strategy, and it will help give a business a unique distinctive advantage, not just an approach to imitate a competitor. A distinctive advantage is what Robert defines as a strategy that "changes the rules of the game in its favor."[19] He further explains that if entrepreneurs enter a business where they are not leaders, then they should "never play the game according to the rules the leader has set." In other words, you will never out-Disney Disneyworld! The only chance you have for success is by creating a distinctive advantage to change the rules of play. For instance, when the Holiday World Theme Park began offering free soft drinks all day, it enjoyed a 20% increase in attendance in a year when other theme parks had a decline.[20]

Find things that are *just not done* in your industry and do them. Spirit Airlines offers inexpensive first-class upgrades. Universal Studios offers VIP "no wait" guest passes. Lexus Dealers offer free car washes for the life of the car. General Motors offers two-day demos on their cars.

"Strategies are the bulldozers. They convert what you want to do into accomplishment."
Peter Drucker

"Strategy is at once, the course we chart, the journey we imagine, and at the same time, it is the course we steer, the trip we actually make."
Fred Nichols

To find the key element in strategic thinking, an entrepreneur must first determine the one driving force of a business venture. Here again, Robert has identified 10 possible driving forces: product/service, user/customer, market/category, production capacity/capability, technology/know how, sales/marketing method, distribution method, natural resources, size/growth, or return/profit. It is important to note that all ten forces could be present in a business venture, but only one is crucial to gain competitive advantage. You must identify that one force![21]

In his book *Good to Great*, Jim Collins describes a similar notion that "great" companies seem to be operating within a Hedgehog Concept (hedgehogs only know one BIG thing). Basically it involves three interacting points:
- What is your business best at in the world?
- What drives the economic engine of your business?
- What is it that your business is passionate about?[22]

Strategic planning, on the other hand, involves tactics. Tactics are the day-to-day operations and activities that implement your strategy. Strategic thinking and strategic planning together bridge the gap between the ends and means of a business.

Consider Grand Dental's unique distinctive advantage utilizing the sales/marketing force. Mark and Maryann Kushube are both entrepreneurial pediatric dentists on the outskirts of Chicago. From the moment you drive up to their office you know this isn't typical dentistry–their sign is a 25-foot toothbrush. As you walk into their high-tech office you're greeted by two animatronic furry characters that sing and tell stories about proper dental care. Dr. Mark is also a magician, with Dr. Maryann as his assistant. They periodically perform on local children's television shows where they "not-so-subtly" pitch their dentistry business. The two also include mini-magic performances as part of making the kids feel at ease during dental visits.

"A business model identifies your customers and describes how your business will profitably address their needs. Strategy, on the other hand, is about differentiating how your business satisfies customers."[23]

43

19. Mission statement

In *The Mission Statement Book,* Jeffrey Abrahams states that: "Every company, no matter how big or small, needs a mission statement as a source of direction, a kind of compass that lets its employees, its customers, and even its stockholders know what it stands for and where it's headed."(25) Abrahams goes on to define a mission statement as "an enduring statement of purpose for an organization that identifies the scope of its operations in product and market terms, and reflects its values and priorities."(26)

A mission statement is basically a brief description that explains what business you're in and why you're in it. It is usually one to three paragraphs long, but it could be as short as a sentence. It is essentially your company's operational philosophy. Consider the following guiding questions when creating a mission statement:

1. What is it that your business does?
2. Why are you in business?
3. What image do you want the world to have about your company?
4. What are your company's values?
5. What are your company's priorities?
6. What is the company's position in the marketplace?
7. How do you differentiate yourself?
8. Who do you plan to do it to?
9. What special qualities will all of this be done within?
10. What is it that makes your business unique?
11. What is the role of the employees?
12. What strategy will you use to achieve the above?

Putting a mission statement together is a thought-provoking experience that requires considerable time and effort. Just experiencing the process will help solidify the reasons for what you're doing, and it will help to examine the personal motives behind your business venture.

There are really no writing rules here! A mission statement represents the heart and soul of your company. It should scream, or speak, or whisper what you are about with the same essence of what you hope to accomplish with your business. It will ultimately serve as an inspiration for you, for management, and for your employees, and it should be a personal commitment to customers, suppliers, the community, and even competitors.

Mission statements are typically one of the hardest things for entrepreneurs to write. Mission statements tell a lot about your business, so it's important to take time, look at some mission statement examples, and put some serious effort into writing a good one. We have a test we use with beginning entrepreneurs and their mission statements–we encourage them to let their parents read it. If they understand the overall business philosophy and can play it back–it works!

Writing a mission statement is really only half the battle. Actually living it on a day-to-day basis is even more difficult. So many times in start-up ventures, there is a real disconnect between writing a mission statement and executing it. It is crucially important that all employees understand and demonstrate the working mission of the company. It should be an inherent part of how they think and perform. According to Eric Shultz, "In today's evolving business environment, not only do you need a clear, succinct, well defined working mission statement for the company, but each department needs to develop its own mission that identifies its role in supporting the company goals." Shultz also says that each employee should develop a personal mission statement by:

1. By simply describing their job activities.
2. Developing a core principle in which to act.
3. Deciding who he/she is working to help.[27]

This is Hallmark. We believe that our products and services must enrich people's lives and enhance their relationships. That creativity and quality in our concepts, products, and services are essential to our success. That the people of Hallmark are our Company's most valuable resource. That distinguished financial performance is a must, not as an end unto itself, but as a means to accomplish our broader mission. That our private ownership must be preserved.

Our mission is to be the best gourmet food and gift company.
      Cheryl&Co.

45

20. The name game

The right name can be an excellent marketing tool. It can also help make your company memorable, and it often can make positioning easier. Because of our background in visual communication, we have always been students of good business names–especially clever ones. Some favorites are an event-planning company called "Taa Daaa" and a second-hand store called "The Way We Wore." But hairstylists seem to be the absolute experts at coming up with "pun" names. Try these on: The Hair After, Cliptomania, Choice Cuts, Hairs Johnny, Now Hair This, Julius Scissors, The Mane Man, and Well-comb All.

So many new products and services have erupted into the marketplace in the last decade that it is not easy to find a truly unique name. Sometimes people pick names that at first seem appropriate, but after they are in the marketplace for a while they seem to lose their luster. Toyota introduced an automobile model in Canada called the Psunami. It quickly and quietly changed the name after the Asian disaster.

The simplest thing to do is use your own name. According Tom Peters, you are in fact a brand. (You might want to add a phrase to clarify what you do.) Many of our personal business ventures are part of a corporation called Poor & Company. And quite frankly, the obvious negative financial connotation has never really come up in any business discussion, and as far as we know, we have never lost any sales because of it.

Jim Wegryn's article on the web, "An Old lady and a Mop"[28] gives the following advice on business names: "So if you are looking for a good name, my advice is to do a little serious cogitation, grab it from the gut, and spend the rest of your time on the object of your christening. Remember, you can not buy a good name–you have to sell it."

The rock. A local restaurant spun off Hard Rock's name and called itself Soft Rock. It stayed small and under Hard Rock's radar for years. As Soft Rock became more successful, the owner decided that he wanted to franchise his idea. He approached Hard Rock's management about keeping the Soft Rock name. They instantly refused to cooperate, and he changed the name to Easystreet. The moral of this story is don't sound too similar especially in the same industry.

Electric t-shirts. A student started a t-shirt silk-screening company that was named The Electric T-shirt Factory. His business boomed, and he decided to venture outside the world of just printing t-shirts. But he found over time that his company name was too limiting and that people didn't think he sold anything but t-shirts. He eventually changed the name to Screen Printed Products, which was a much better way of describing the company's expertise.

46

Identity is everything 21.

Image isn't something–it's everything. The quality of your image can mean the difference between success and failure. It can be that simple and that deadly. The overall visual image that your business conveys to the world should be in harmony with your company's vision and philosophy. That visual image is generally referred to as your identity program or design platform.

The cornerstone of the identity program is the logo or trademark (or service mark for a service company). A successful logo is a means of condensing a complex reality into a single, simple statement that is an indication of the overall quality, value, reliability, and differentiation of a business. The logo is generally the most charged design element of a company, and its main objective is to identify the company clearly, instantaneously, and memorably–on both the cognitive and emotional levels of the public. The logo should be able to build a positive, strong, and long-lasting impression on existing and prospective customers. The moment people view your logo, they should instantly think of your company. Think Nike. That is what branding is all about!

The key elements to an identity program are the company's name, logo, tag line, and color. Once developed, these components are used consistently on your stationery, envelopes, business cards, advertising messages, signage, vehicles, apparel, packaging, literature, web site, promotional items, newsletters, annual reports, exhibitry, and business plan.

An excellent way to prepare yourself for the task of developing an identity program is to study successful ones from other companies. Our favorites are Apple Computer, FedEx, Pepsi, Coke, and McDonalds. You'll notice that the secret to developing an effective identity program is simplicity. Keep your overall image simple. Think Apple, IBM, and Nike.

Plumbing. When we first moved to town, we met a young entrepreneur named Neil Gearhart who was starting a plumbing company. we approached him about developing an identity package for his business, and he reluctantly agreed as he didn't really believe it was necessary. Now some thirty years later, he would point to the company logo as one of things that brought him so much success. His blue trucks with the Gearhart wrench logo are instantly recognizable in the community.

If you have the graphic design skill, you might want to develop your own identity program–providing you have the time. Most people should spend the money to have it professionally prepared as it is obviously money well worth investing. Good sources for on-line graphic design firms are Portfolio.com., Elance.com., and Logodesignguru.com

Somewhere along the way, you might wish to protect your company's image from others using a confusingly similar mark through trademark registration. The first step in the process is to establish if there is a similar company using the same name. If you decide to pursue registration, we recommend that you hire a professional attorney who specializes in that legal arena. But keep in mind that this is not inexpensive proposition.

We had a professional trademark search done for a 3-D animation company called Lifeforms–which designed and fabricated animatronic characters. The search found a number of different companies using the Lifeform name and one that appeared to be doing 3-D computer animation–a similar concept name but an entirely different product and production process. But because there could be potential product confusion, we changed the name to Lifeformations (actually a better name for what the company does). A new search for Lifeformations turned up no other companies with that name. The entire search and application process has cost over $25,000–with yearly charges for ongoing miscellaneous filing fees.

The navy. Tom Cousino opened a new, local restaurant called the Old Navy Bistro a few years ago. Everything was fine until the national Old Navy clothing store came to town. Typically there would have been no problem because one was a restaurant and the other was a clothing store. The law states that as long as there could be no customer confusion between the companies using the name it would be acceptable. But Tom was selling shirts and hats with the name Old Navy on them. Tom had to change his restaurant's name because the Old Navy clothing store owned the trademark rights.

Marketing plan **22.**

Marketing is a concept designed to increase customer awareness and deliver a businesses message. A marketing plan is the strategy you will use to get your customers. It is your sales plan of action that contains your goals, tactics, and media. It includes what you will sell, to whom you will sell it, at what price, and how will you get the product to the customer.

In her book, *Start Your Own Business,* Rieva Lesonsky suggests three steps for putting together effective marketing plans:

Step 1. Define your product. Fully understand the features and benefits of your product as compared to the competition. Differentiation and competitive advantage must be clearly defined and understood. Pricing and positioning must be analyzed and processed.

Step 2. Describe your target audience. Develop a demographic profile of your target audience. Know as much about them as you possibly can. Walk in their shoes. Where do they shop? How often to they buy what you sell? Are there peak buying periods?

Step 3. Create a communication strategy. The goal here is to get your customers' attention. What do they read? What do they listen to? What do they watch? How often do they need to experience your message (repetition)? Ultimately, your communication solution plan should include everything from your logo design and advertising to pubic relations and promotions.*(29)*

The average business spends between 3-5% of its gross sales on advertising. For some businesses that is too much money; for others, it won't be enough. For a start-up, you'll have to base your advertising budget on your market survey or what you learned from the industry and competitor research.

Wrigley's Gum. There is a story that circulates about the chewing gum tycoon Wrigley. He was riding on a train in Europe when someone recognized him and asked, "Why if you sold more gum than anyone on earth, would you keep advertising like you do?" Wrigley's response was, "How fast do you think we are going on this train?" The man answered, "I'm not sure, but probably 70 miles per hour." Wrigley replied, "Would you shut the engine off?"

B2B. For businesses that sell to other businesses, we're a big fan of trade shows as one of their primary marketing techniques. The big strength of trade shows is that the customers come to you. There weakness is that most of your competitors are there as well. But if you have done your differentiation homework, that won't be a problem–just a selling opportunity. Trade shows have also taught us the importance of recognizing how long the buying process can take–sometimes years for big-ticket items (things that cost a bundle).

Marketing, advertising, and public relations. We used to have a difficult time distinguishing those terms from each other until we heard this little saying: If you were going downtown to find a date and you told a potential squeeze about your great car, how much money you made and your fancy crib–that would be advertising. If you were to tell him/her how far you two would go in life together, what great-looking kids you would make, and how wonderful life would be together–that would be marketing. If he/she went out with you because they heard all that stuff from the bartender–that would be public relations.

A lot of college marketing programs teach the 4 "P's" of marketing: Product, Pricing, Promotion, and Placement. But there are a lot more P's out here that they could add, including: Publicity, Packaging, and Premiums.

Just like most facets of running a start-up business, your initial marketing efforts have a lot to do with playing your hunches and with good old trial and error. You quickly learn what works and what doesn't and where you get your biggest media return on investment. But be aware: once you open your doors for business, you'll be swamped with dozens of advertising opportunities. Having your marketing plan in hand will help you fend them off.

Once you have established your niche or target audience, it becomes easier to identify what your "media mix" will ultimately be. The "media mix" is how you divide your advertising dollars among different media. You obviously have a lot of options for your media dollar. Here is a list of some of the more common media methods:

1. Print ads–magazines and newspapers
2. Radio
3. Television
4. Direct mail
5. Fliers
6. Brochures
7. Catalogs
8. Newsletters
9. Classifieds
10. Web sites
11. Trade shows
12. Promotional items
13. Phone books
14. Signage
15. Public relations articles

Repetition is the foundation of advertising programs. Some studies indicate that you have to expose potential customers to your marketing message nearly 30 times for them to purchase from your business. Now what do you think about starting a business? If it were easy–everyone would do it!

Selling 23.

There's an old saying that "nothing happens unless something is sold." Managers won't manage. Designers won't design. Producers won't produce, and teachers won't teach. You probably wouldn't be reading this book if someone hadn't sold you on the idea. Few products sell themselves. Most have to be sold. Selling is key to the world of business and getting things to happen.

Thousands of books have been written on selling, and every one of them probably has some unique words of wisdom. But all of them include the three main points of the selling process: prospecting, presenting, and closing.

Selling is perhaps the greatest skill of all time. The ability to persuade, communicate, and influence has been the basis of personal and business success throughout the ages. But it takes a certain type of individual to master those skills. And because those skills remain somewhat nebulous and mysterious, sales people are often referred to as rainmakers. Think you have it? Consider this:

A survey by Amanda Ruth and Allen Wysocki[30] of the top hot- selling companies generated the following sales person attributes:

1. **Knowledge.** Overall product knowledge and the ability to deliver the right amount of information for the client to understand.
2. **Enthusiasm.** The ability to give all that it takes for a client to take notice.
3. **Integrity.** Honest, strong positive work ethics; responsiveness; and the ability to solve problems.
4. **Persistence.** The fortitude to never give up or doubt your ability to close the deal.
5. **Relationships.** The ability to be liked and to develop a win-win position.

"The art of selling goods is as difficult to acquire as any art. The proper methods can be acquired only by a multiplicity of actual experiments, and the one who tries the greatest variety of experiments will become, finally, a master of the art."

Tom Edison

6. Fun. The ability to demonstrate that you love what you're doing (and so will the client).

No matter what they're selling, great salespeople share some common traits. They:

1. Are entrepreneurial. They see themselves running a business within a business.
2. Have developed a personal selling process that works best for them.
3. Think about customers, not quotas. They focus solely on the customer and the customer's needs.
4. Sell solutions. They clearly focus on solving customer problems.
5. Get customers thinking. They begin the closing process immediately.
6. Aren't afraid to get creative. They think sales is show business.
7. Are on the move. They constantly find reasons to meet with customers.
8. Know when to move on. They instinctively recognize dead ends.
9. Stay current. They know what is happening with customers, products, trends, and the competition.
10. Treat everyone as a potential customer.
11. Know that customers don't care about them.
12. Love what they do. They have passion!

Rainmaker. We met a young aggressive sales person a number of years ago who was selling big-ticket items–million-dollar equipment. We didn't want his product, but we wanted to know his story because he was incredible at selling. He told us that he had just graduated and had gotten his job with a Fortune 500 company by demonstrating his ability to close. At the end of the his interview, he was asked if he had any questions and he replied, "When do I start and where do I park?" The interviewer was so surprised by his response–which was really him asking for the sale. He got the job!

In the final analysis, everyone in a business needs to know that they are salespeople. The entire organization is actually involved in a continuous selling process. From the receptionist to the phone operator (if they're smart enough to have one), to the technical representatives, to the service department, to the greeter, to the cook, to accounts receivable–anyone who comes in contact with your customer makes an impression about your product and service. Sales is like Gestalt psychology. The sum is greater than the individual parts.

Decisions, decisions, decisions 24.

Selecting the right legal framework for your business is one of the most important decisions you must make before actually launching the company. All businesses operate under one of four legal classifications: sole proprietorship, partnership, corporation, or limited liability company. The decision is basically driven by the overall objectives of the entrepreneur and the possible business investors.

The structure you choose for the business will affect many things including your personal legal liability, taxes, and how profits are dispersed among the owners. The choice is made difficult by trade-offs built into the laws governing businesses. For instance, to get the best tax benefits, a business must give up flexibility or some protection from liability or both. Let's take a closer look at the advantages and disadvantages of each of the classifications.

Sole proprietorship: This is a business owned by one person with no formal legal structure. The advantage is that it is simple to do. (You're already in business–you just own 100% of nothing.) You probably will have to seek a local business license. You file your business taxes as part of your personal income taxes with an additional form called Schedule "C." The disadvantage is that you have no personal liability protection. If your business gets sued, you could lose everything you own.

Partnership: A partnership is similar to a sole proprietorship except there is more than one owner who actively engages in the management of the company. The advantage is the same as a sole proprietorship in that there are no legal forms–possibly just a licence. Profits and losses flow directly to the owner's personal tax forms. The disadvantage is that each partner has unlimited personal liability, even for each other. Note that partnerships come in two varieties–general and limited. In a general partnership, all partners manage the business (not necessarily at the same time) and assume all responsibilities and debt. The limited partnership has both general and limited partners. The general partners have the same obligations as above, while the limited partners serve only as investors–having no control of the business and no exposure to the liabilities.

Limited Liability Company (LLC): This has become the form of choice for many small start-up companies. An LLC combines many of the best features of a partnership and a corporation. They are typically formed under a state LLC statute which requires that an Articles of Organization be filed with the Secretary of State and that the LLC's owners enter into an Operating Agreement. The advantages include personal liability protection for all the owners, pass-through profits without corporate taxation, and a more flexible profit distribution system. The disadvantage is that they are more complicated to establish than a sole proprietorship or partnership, hence requiring additional legal assistance.

"C" Corporation: A "C" corporation is synonymous with the common definition of a corporation. It is an entity chartered by the state and treated as a person under law. The advantages include that there are no limits to the number of people who can own stock, the participants personally have no liability, and that this is the legal form of a company that could be publicly traded. The disadvantages include double taxation–once at a corporate rate and again at the individual's personal level.

"S" Corporation: An "S" Corporation is similar to a "C" corporation in that it is by definition a corporation. The main advantage is that there is no double taxation in that the profits/losses are distributed directly to the stockholders at their percentage of ownership and are only taxed at that individual's rate. The disadvantage is that venture capitalist partnerships cannot be stockholders.

Issues	Sole Proprietorship	Partnership	S-Corporation	C-Corporation	Limited Liability Company
Liability	Owner and business are liable.	Owners and business are liable. However, Limited Partners are liable to only amount invested.	Shareholders have limited liability.	Shareholders have limited liability.	Members have limited liability.
Tax	Profit and losses flow directly to owner's personal tax return.	Each partner reports income on their personal tax return.	Profits and losses flow through to share-holder's personal tax returns on percentage of ownership.	Corporation pays its own tax and share-holders pay tax on their dividends.	Profits and losses flow through to member's personal tax returns on percentage of ownership.
Management	Owner.	Shared by partners per prior agreement.	Shared by shareholders.	Shared by shareholders.	Shared by members.
Life of Business	Terminates on owner's death or sale.	Unless stipulated in partner's agreement, termination on death or withdrawal.	Corporations have a life of their own.	Corporations have a life of their own.	Check with the residing state's regulations
Set-up	Easy to form–possible license required.	A formal agreement and legal counsel is highly recommended.	Filing is required through state government.	Filing is required through state government.	Filing is required through state government.

25. Employees

At some point, if your one-person entrepreneurial business is really successful, you will probably need to hire your first employee. Trust us—nothing changes the dynamics of the experience more than an employee. Instantly, you will need a job description, a payroll procedure, and employee policies on such items as vacations, sick days, work times, and quality/performance standards.

It is not the intention of this book to even pretend that we can present the necessary information regarding the challenges of bringing your first employee on board. But we would like to share some of our experiences regarding new hires:

- They can simply make or break your business.
- They're either solving problems or they are a problem.
- They're either making you money or costing you money.
- You will either pay them what they think they are worth or they will steal the difference in time, productivity, product, and/or money.
- The higher the skill level required, the more difficult it is to find the perfect employee.
- If there are now two of you–the new hire makes up 50% of your company and can cause at least that percentage of problems.
- No matter what problems they cause or stupid decisions they make, they expect to be paid on time.
- There is no such thing as buying loyalty.
- Every penny you pay them is money you could be paying yourself, so be sure you really need to hire someone.
- Understand that the conditions you start them out with become a standard or "normal," and very few employees will allow you to take anything away.
- If at first you see a little negative characteristic in them, you'll see a lot of it before it's over.

Management 26.

Whenever we ask up-and-coming entrepreneurs, "Which would you rather do–be told what to do or tell somebody what to do?" The majority will answer, "Tell somebody!" Their answer screams of not knowing or understanding much about the reality of management. Managing is typically a tough, demanding, hectic, and grueling occupation that can be rewarding for a few people with the right "people" skills and personality traits. But management is surely not a career position for everyone.

In a nutshell, management is getting people to do what needs to be done at the quality required and in the time allotted. Managers are leaders, coaches, counselors, cheerleaders, and therapists–to name a few characteristics. A more scholarly definition can be found in Robert Kreitner's textbook entitled *Management(31)*. Kreitner states that management is "the process of working with and through others to achieve organizational objectives in a changing environment. Central to this process is the effective and efficient use of limited resources." And nowhere will resources be more limited than in an entrepreneur's start-up venture.

The question, "What do managers actually do?" can be answered two ways–through their functions and their roles. The functional approach is based on early work by a French industrialist named Henry Fayol, and it includes planning, decision making, organizing, staffing, communicating, motivating, leading, and controlling. The role approach is the work of Henri Mintzberg, and those qualities are grouped into the following three categories: interpersonal, informational, and decisional.

A corporate executive was once asked, "What makes a great leader?" His answer was: "Great followers! " So what characteristics do great followers look for in managers? A study conducted by the Learning-Leadership Development

Committee[32] identified the following twelve characteristics of effective managers:

1. They see the success before it happens.
2. They hold a vision.
3. They look for ideas that excite others.
4. They pick ideas that are contagious.
5. They think big and long term.
6. They believe others have important contributions to make.
7. They coach.
8. They counsel.
9. They encourage others to do well.
10. They set high expectations and maintain them.
11. They make extensive use of polite words and phrases.
12. They value people and relationships.

Tom Peters says it best in his book *Re-imagine*[33], when he describes leadership as:

- *Joyous*–by marshaling the talents of others to a seriously cool cause.
- *Horrible*–by having to sort through the mess of human relations.
- *Cool*–an adventure that enables us to magnify our impact on the world.
- *Lonely*–a constant battle of doubt and dread with only your own judgement about human nature to rely on.
- *Different*–emphasis on inspiring excellence, not doing.
- *The ultimate responsibility*–it's an assumption of accountability over people you cannot control and actions you don't perform.
- *Not what you think*–it's not about command and control but living in the depths and soaring to the heights ("rallying others to invent and then pursue seemingly impossible dreams").

We remember hearing Steven Jobs once say that really good people are self-managing. They instinctively know what to do. Their only real need is to work with people that they can learn from. When we initially formed Lifeformations, we put together a team of five really talented people. Steven was right. They were all self-managing (maybe one wasn't–but what he lacked in managing himself he made up in skill). All we had to add to the group was a vision!

Pricing 27.

Pricing your product or service is one of the most important issues facing an entrepreneur. Although there are formulas that can be used as guides, pricing remains more an art than a science. Pricing something too low can signal an inferior product or service, while pricing it too high may put it above the target customer's price point. In the final analysis, customers pay the price that is consistent with their perceived value of the product or service. If the name on the product or service is perceived as having a high value (such as Lexus), then the customer may be willing to pay a premium price.

Selecting the right price is the result of a number of variables:

- **Your niche audience.** How much do they now pay for a similar product or service?
- **Your perceived value.** How will your target customers perceive what you're offering in terms of quality and value?
- **Your competition's offering.** What are your competitors charging? How are they perceived in terms of quality and value?
- **What are your total costs?** Be sure you have identified your total product or service costs. Hidden cost are business breakers.
- **Profit.** You need to make a profit on everything you sell. Many beginners believe you can make it up on volume. Nothing times "high" volume is still nothing.
- **Sales projections.** What monetary sales goals have you projected? The best price will obviously generate the most sales. But the best price won't generate the best margin. Small margins require the entrepreneur to sell more in order to cover the overhead. There is an old saying that sums this up: "Double your price, half of your customers will go away, you'll be home in time for supper, and make the same amount of money."

Antiques. You can learn a lot about pricing by going to an antique show that has lots of dealers. But for the best lesson, you have to go very early in the morning before most of the regular customers arrive. Early is when the "smart" dealers roam around the site buying from other dealers–specifically items that they think that the other dealer has priced too low. The smart dealers know the market and what it will bear. They are also scoping out the show to see how many of the same antiques are being sold. The more commodity-like the antique, the more price sensitive the market will be. Too many of the same items will drive the price down. They also know that a unique antique can be priced at whatever they like.

Messing with price.
Disney and Universal
have both been attempt-
ing to see just how
much they can charge
theme park customers
before it starts to reduce
attendance. Obviously,
there are a number of
factors that also could
affect attendance such
as weather, economy,
and competition. But
both of these parks
have been around long
enough to factor in most
of those variables. As
they inched their gate
fees up, it appeared that
the maximum price
point was about $50.00
a day. So both parks
have hovered around
that number for the
last couple of years.
In order to raise that
number over $50.00,
they'll have to increase
the perceived value.
One popular way of
doing that would be by
adding additional thrill
rides or attractions,
but that would require
an additional major
expense. Here is where
the internal financial
wizards start calculating
the cost/benefit analysis
computations.

• **Other considerations.** Wholesale allowances, quantity discounts, credit card charges, and offering extended credit will also affect pricing decisions.

Entrepreneurs typically use one of three different techniques in determining their prices:

• **Cost-based pricing** is determined by adding a standard or arbitrary mark-up to the product or service cost.

• **Market-based pricing** is determined by mirroring what the competition is charging for a similar product or service.

• **Value-based pricing** is determined by estimating what customers are willing to pay based on their perceived value of the product or service. That perception can be manipulated through branding, positioning, and similar marketing techniques.

Studying the industry your business is in will give you some insight into how prices are established. For instance, the restaurant industry uses an average food cost of 25% and a liquor cost of 18% for a typical full-service sit-down establishment. Many retail-type businesses work on a 100% mark-up practice, whereas jewelry stores can reach 200% or more. By identifying approximate mark-up percentages, start-up entepreneurs can get some idea of what the competition might be working with in terms of gross margins.

We recently heard how some professional apartment owners establish their rental prices. They typically set a goal for a 95% occupancy rate. If occupancy drops below 95%, they are charging too much for the apartment. If their occupancy rate goes above 95%, they are charging too little. Naturally this system works best with large apartment complexes and may not work in all areas of the country. But it is a clever system to study as a way of establishing the ideal rental price.

Service businesses don't get paid for all the hours that they actually work. Their employees may "put in" 50 hours a week but get paid for only 30 "billable" hours that they can charged directly to a customer. Establishing an hourly rate for a service business is as complex as pricing a product.

A common way is to first determine how much money you want to make for a year. Let's use Kate's space-organizing business as an example. She has decided that she would like to gross $35,000 a year to start. There are 2,080 working hours in a year (40 x 52). She figures that she will spend a third of that time (690 hours) selling her services and two-thirds of that time (1,380 hours) actually organizing someone's home, apartment or business. Most of her expenses will be passed through to her clients, but she will have about $8,000 worth of business expenses for a grand total of $43,000. Dividing $43,000 by 1,380 billable hours has her hourly rate at roughly $30.00.

Now that Kate knows her hourly rate, she really has two ways to work with clients–hourly or by the project.
- **Hourly** is where she bills the clients for the exact amount of hours it takes her to perform the service. Kate prefers this technique as it is an open checkbook.
- **Project** is where she gives a fixed amount of money to complete the task based on her estimate of hours required times her hourly rate. Clients prefer this way as they know what the total cost will be up front.

Now the big question is how Kate's rate compares to others in the area performing similar activities. That $30.00 an hour rate not only has to satisfy Kate's personal requirements but also compare favorably to the competition in terms of similar services rendered. In the final analysis, will the market be willing to pay that much for her service?

But what about a business that has two or more people employed? How do you figure that hourly rate? Let's take a look at a start-up communication technology business.

"Remember, everything communicates some-thing to consumers about your product. This is especially true of pric-ing. The price you are ask makes a statement about the value you are offering the consumer. If you are offering a low price, consumers assume you have a modest opinion of the value of your goods. If you offer a high price, consumers infer that your product has high value and that it truly delivers on the benefits."

Eric Schultz[34]

61

Phillis and Jenna decide to go into the web site design and development business. Phillis will be on the road selling, and Jenna will design and produce the actual sites. Phillis and Jenna would both like to make $75,000 a year or $36.00 an hour. They both will work out of Jenna's garage and have minimal overhead expenses of approximately $10,000 a year. Their total yearly expenses are $160,000.

In order for Phillis to sell their web site services, she needs to establish what their hourly billable time should be. The only real billable time of this partnership is Jenna as she is the person responsible for the actual web site production. (Jenna simply has to carry Phillis.) Consequently, if this were a perfect world, she would simply divide $160,000 by 2,080 work hours in a year (40 hours x 52 weeks). Their billable rate would be about $76.00 an hour. But hold on! It isn't a perfect world. Not even close.

Jenna wants some vacation, sick time, and personal time off. So let's subtract 160 hours from 2,080 and we have 1,920 remaining. But even when Jenna is working, she isn't always productive in that she has clean-up and maintenance activities to perform at least an hour a day. So we can subtract another 260 hours (52 x 5) from 1,920 and have 1,660 hours remaining. But Phillis isn't always effective at selling Jenna's time, so let's subtract another 200 hours and have 1,460 hours billable remaining. Dividing $160,000 by 1460 hours gives us a billable hourly charge of approximately $110.00 an hour. That's a far cry from the $36.00 an hour that Phillis and Jenna each make.

Here again, pricing is yet another reason that entrepreneurs ought to work within the industry first before starting out on their own. Just being inside the business gives you an excellent vantage point to analyze the costs and pricing considerations.

Location x three 28.

When it comes to retail, three of the most important considerations are: location, location, and location. Beyond that age old advice, do you want to be in a downtown area, an indoor mall, an outdoor strip mall, a popular street, or off the beaten path?

Roy Williams in his book *The Wizard of Ads*[35] refers to a great location for a retail business as one that has intrusive visibility. Intrusive visibility means that people see you when they're not looking for you. Intrusive visibility means the average person can immediately picture the building and/or location when you casually mention its location. Williams believes that "intrusive visibility is not always available, but when you can get it, it's worth all the money you have to pay."

Manufacturing, production, and service businesses have different priorities to consider, and the very nature of the activity generally dictates the kind of facility and location requirements. It is possible to "bootstrap" some of these activities out of the home, but most zoning codes prohibit having any outside employees even if they allow the venture to take place within the dwelling.

The best advice is to contact a commercial real estate broker and see what is available for your idea. Once you establish what properties are being offered, do your homework to evaluate the suitability of your idea to the various locations. We firmly adhere to the notion of staying in as small a facility as possible. We don't believe in growing into a place. It seldom happens. Customers think you're struggling when there is unused space with no activity. It spooks them into believing you're on the brink of going under.

" Close quarters can charge the dynamics of a hot group. One of our hottest studio teams meets for its biweekly lunch in a ridiculously cramped space, and I doubt that the intensity would be the same if the room weren't so crowded. Too much square footage like too much budget can dissipate energy and discourage a more immediate and emotional connection between team members."
Tom Kelley[36]

29. Show me the money!

Stan Laurel and Oliver Hardy decided to go into the watermelon business. The two of them borrow a friend's truck and drive to Florida. They buy a 100 watermelons for a buck each and drive back home. They set up their stand on a corner and begin selling watermelons for, yes, a buck each. After they sold them all and counted their money, they realized that they had the same amount of money as they started with (which is pretty amazing in that there was no waste, had to buy gas, and that they sold all of them). So with the absence of any PROFIT, Stanley says to Oliver, "I told you we should have gotten a bigger truck!" Insert laughter here!

Pretty silly story, right? The fact is that millions of people lost a fortune in the last few years investing into dot com businesses that had no profit potential, either. There was no basic business model present, but still people invested, hoping for the big return or that all the "high-techies" really needed was the equivalent of a bigger truck.

A lot of entrepreneurs find financial information absolutely painful. That's probably why 80% of new businesses fail within the first five years. And worst yet, 80% of the remaining 20% fail within the next five years.

The fact is, you can't plan or run a successful business without knowing exactly what your financial situation is at any given point in time. You simply need to know the four building blocks of business finances: the income statement, the balance sheet, the cash flow statement, and the break-even point. These four pieces of information will give you a pretty complete snapshot of how you're doing or will do. In spite of what many people think, these are really very elementary calculations–just simple math.

The **income statement** (also called a profit-and-loss statement, a P&L, or an earnings report) basically tells how much money you made over a certain time period of time minus all your expenses to arrive at a net profit. Simply stated, an income statement tells you if you're making money, breaking even, or losing money. In other words–this tells the reader if your profitable or not.

The **balance sheet** is basically a financial snapshot of your business at a particular period of time–usually at the end of the year. It's divided into a top half and bottom half. The top half includes everything you own that has monetary value (called your assets). The bottom half includes everything you owe (called liabilities) together with what your company is worth (called your equity). The top and bottom halves always have to be in balance, hence the name balance sheet–get it? Simply stated, a balance sheet tells you how financially strong you are in terms of weathering a possible monetary storm. In other words–this tells the reader what you own and what you owe.

The **cash flow statement** tracks the cash as it flows in and out of the business over a given period of time. It too is divided into a top and bottom half. The top half is cash coming in from various sources, The bottom half is cash going out to various sources, such as labor, cost of goods, vendors, etc. This form has to balance at the top and bottom halves as well. Simply stated, a cash flow statement tells you how much cash you have on hand. In other words–this tells the reader how liquid your business is.

The **break-even point** is the most important factor entrepreneurs can know about their business venture. It is the point when they have sold enough product or performed enough services to cover their expenses. It is the point at which a business starts making a profit.

30. Income statement

Whenever business people talk about the bottom line–they're probably talking about what is revealed in the income statement. By adding up all your income and subtracting all your expenses, the income statement reveals your net profit.

Revenue – Expenses = Net Profit

To get an idea of how an income statement works, let's take a look at a teddy bear retail store called Everything Fluffy for the most recent year.

		Everything Fluffy Income Statement	
		01/01/04 - 12/31/04	
1.		Revenue in-store	325,000
		Revenue catalog	+450,000
	Gross Revenue	-	**775,000**
2.		Cost of goods sold	-455,000
	Gross Profits		**+320,000**
3.		Sales, general, & Administration	-180,000
		Depreciation	-15,000
	Operating Profit		**+125,000**
4.		Dividend & Interest Income	+0
		Interest Expense	-12,000
	Profit Before Taxes		**+113,000**
5.		Taxes	-27,000
	Net Profit		**+86,000**

Section 1, the **gross revenue section** refers to any income that the business takes in as a direct result of operating the venture. "Gross" refers to the fact that no expenses have been subtracted from that number whatsoever. Depending on the business, this section could include revenue streams from rent, product sales, services rendered, internet sales, etc. Break them out as needed for your understanding.

Everything Fluffy sells its product (teddy bears) two ways– through a retail store and a catalog. When they get their web page up and running, that will be a third entry in the gross revenue section called internet sales. As you can see, they did pretty well with sales of $775,000.

Section 2, the **gross profits section** refers to the money you can keep (kind of) after all the expenses are taken out. Generally you take out any expenses that are directly related to the product or service being rendered. This is a category where you and your accountant have to make a judgment call on exactly what components are to be considered "direct." When you do decide, then stay consistent over time with those costs. Break those costs out as needed for a better understanding.

Everything Fluffy had a total cost of goods sold of $455,000. That number included the labor costs directly related to selling the product, the wholesale cost of the product, and the shipping costs in receiving the product from the manufacturer. After those costs were subtracted from $775,000, the store had a gross profit of $320,000.

Section 3, the **operating profit** section refers to the money you can keep after the remaining non direct expenses are taken out. These include advertising, travel, telephone, utilities, rent, your salary, secretary's salary, bookkeeping, automobile, accountant and legal fees, etc. Again some of these expenses could be lumped with the above section based on a judgment call. The idea here in separating them is to give you a snapshot of where your expenses are going and where to trim costs if necessary.

Everything Fluffy had a total of $180,000 in sales, general and administrative. The depreciation of $15,000 was on various pieces of computer equipment, store display cases, and a retail storefront building that are being written off over their respective lifetimes.

Section 4, the **profit before taxes section** refers to the money you can keep before taxes are paid. These have to be kept out of your income and expense section because they are not part of your day-to-day business operations. For instance, you may be fortunate enough as a new business owner to accumulate some cash and want to invest it for interest income–this is where that is shown. This is also where your interest on loans you borrowed shows up on your income statement as well.

Everything Fluffy had no investments that made any income. They do have interest expense for two bank loans: one short term for equipment and the other long term for the building.

Section 5, the **net profit section** refers to the income that you actually can call your own–the bottom line. This is the amount you have left after the taxes are paid. Depending on the structure of your company, your business may not directly have to pay taxes because these may funnel directly down to the owner, as in the case of a sole proprietorship.

Balance sheet 31.

A balance sheet gives you a snapshot of what your company is worth at a particular time. (If you ever apply for a personal loan from a bank, they'll ask you to create a similar document on yourself.) For a balance sheet, you tally up everything you own, and that's known as your assets. Then you tally up everything you owe someone else, and that's known as your liabilities. By subtracting your liabilities from your assets, you get your company's net worth or equity.

$$Equity = Assets - Liabilities$$

Unfortunately, accountants have come up with their own "fundamental equation of accounting" which means the same thing, but is confusing as the dickens:

$$Assets = Liabilities + Owner's\ Equity$$

We present the second equation because accountants use it to lay out the balance sheet. The top half of the sheet is your asset section, and the bottom half is your liabilities and owner's equity section. Given the "fundamental equation," the two halves must be equal. Referring to the chart on the next page:

Section 1 describes the company's **current assets** that have monetary value. One of the main things a balance sheet does is show how liquid your assets are. A liquid asset is one that can be converted to cash quickly, generally within a year. Liquid assets include such things as cash, stock, accounts receivable, and inventory. If you're a manufacturer, you would include raw materials, work-in-process, and finished goods. Current assets are very important because they represent the readily available reserves that you can draw from to run your day-to-day operation and fund any unforeseen emergencies.

As you can see, Everything Fluffy has $150,000 in cash and

69

Everything Fluffy
Balance Sheet

	Assets	**2004**
1	**Current Assets**	
	Cash	150,000
	Inventory	+40,000
	Total Current Assets	**190,000**
2	**Fixed Assets**	
	Land/Building	160,000
	Equipment	+14,000
	Accumulated Depreciation	- 40,000
	Total Fixed Assets	**134,000**
3	**Total Assets**	**324,000**

Liabilities and Owner's Equity

4	**Current Liabilities**	
	Accounts Payable	11,000
	Accrued Accounts Payable	+4,200
	Total Current Liabilities	**15,200**
5	**Long Term Liabilities**	
	Building Mortgage	120,000
	Equipment Loan	+8,000
	Total Long Term Liabilities	**128,000**
6	**Owner's Equity**	
	Invested Capital	50,000
	Accumulated Retained Earnings	130,800
	Total Owner's Equity	**180,800**
7	**TOTAL LIABILITIES & EQUITY**	**324,000**

$40,000 in teddy bear inventory, for a grand total of $190,000.

Section 2 describes the **fixed assets,** which are usually larger and last a lot longer–and are not very liquid. Buildings, automobiles, vans, machinery, computers, and the like fall in this category. These kinds of things usually take more than a year to convert into cash.

Everything Fluffy owns its building and the equipment in it. The accumulated depreciation is on those items for the past three years and is subtracted from the amounts above in that section.

Section 3 describes the **total assets** which sum up the current, fixed, and intangible assets.

Everything Fluffy has total assets worth $324,000.

Section 4 describes the **current liabilities,** which include all the monetary obligations that are due within one year. This would include short-term loans, notes on lines of credit, accounts payable to suppliers, and any short-term debt or taxes. Accrued accounts payable items are those amounts that the business knows it owes but has not yet been billed for, such as electricity, phone, and gas.

Everything Fluffy currently owes the teddy bear manufacturer $11,000 that it has received an invoice for, and $4,200 in estimated, miscellaneous amounts that it has not received a bill for but are in fact owed.

Section 5 describes the **long-term liabilities,** which include any monetary obligations that are not due for at least a year. This would include bank debt or any other loan mechanisms.

Everything Fluffy has a ten-year mortgage on the building and a five-year loan on the equipment.

Section 6 describes the **owner's equity** which represents the total amount invested by the stockholders plus the accumulated profit of the business.

Everything Fluffy was started with an initial loan of $50,000 by the owner. Over the last few months, the store has accumulated a profit of $130,800, and it is being retained as earnings within the company.

Section 7 describes the **total liabilities and equity** which sums up the total value of the current and long-term liabilities and then adds on the total owner's equity. Both the top and bottom halves should be in balance.

Cash flow statement 32.

Cash is the name of the game. Cash is the most important part of staying in business. It's literally more important than profit. You don't need to make a profit if you have cash. **Don't misunderstand what I'm saying; profit is an essential part of long-term business survival.** But if you don't have cash, you won't be in business long enough to realize a profitable business.

The instrument businesses use to monitor their cash needs is called a **cash flow statement**. It simply monitors the money coming in and the money going out over a period of time. The typical statement is divided into two halves. The top half keeps track of where the money comes in from and what it goes out for. The bottom half traces where the funds end up (if there are any left) after they're inside your company. The top and bottom sections must be in balance.

Let's take a look at a cash flow statement for this year and last year for our teddy bear store–Anything Fluffy. By comparing two different years, we can monitor how their cash position has changed over time. Since Anything Fluffy's clientele pay either by cash or credit card; their cash flow into the business should be relatively strong, and it is for both years.

Section 1 describes the actual money coming into your business that gets deposited into the checkbook. We're talking cash here–real money coming into your company. This would include "receipts on sales" that were actually received on in-store and catalog transactions. Section 1 would also include any dividend or interest monies that were deposited as well as any capital that the owners might have to invest in the business. If the business sold off any of its assets, the amount of cash received would also show up in this section.

Everything Fluffy accepts cash, check, and credit cards for

It's all about zeroes. We were consulting for a small company in Toledo, Ohio, and the financial controller stopped us in the hall and quietly said, "I got a check in the mail today for $16,000, I have a payroll due tomorrow for $20,000 and I have no other money in the checkbook." We stood there and thought, we also own a business and have a payroll due tomorrow for $3,500.00 and we only have $3,000. And we bet the paper boy in town has a bill due with the daily paper in town probably for $10.00, and he's only collected $7.00. And GM probably has a payroll due tomorrow, and they're short 10 million. And our government has a payroll due tomorrow, and they're short a billion. We're all in the same "cash" boat, with just a different amount of zeros. Cash-on-hand or working capital is the life blood of any business.

Everything Fluffy Cash Flow Statement		
2004		
Inflow and Outflow	**2004**	**2003**
1. Funds Provided By:		
Receipts on in-store sales	325,000	285,000
Receipts on catalog sales	+450,000	+425,000
Dividend and Interest income	-0-	-0-
Invested capital	-0-	-0-
Total Funds In	**775,000**	**710,000**
2. Funds Used For:		
Cost of goods acquired	455,000	411,000
Sales, General & Administration	180,000	180,000
Interest Expense	12,000	12,000
Building and equipment	6,000	6,000
Long-term debt reduction	4,000	2,000
Distribution to owners	20,000	15,000
Total Funds Out:	**677,000**	**626,000**
3. NET CHANGE IN CASH POSITION	**98,000**	**84,000**
Changes By Account	**Last Year**	**Prev. Year**
4. Changes in Liquid Assets		
Cash	98,000	84,000
Investment portfolio	-0-	-0-
Total Changes	**98,000**	**84,000**
5. Net Change In Cash Position	**+98,000**	**+84,000**

product payment. All three of these payments are immediate and are directly deposited into the checkbook nightly. Everything Flufffy had no other income either year. The store did show an increase in total sales of $65,000.

Section 2 describes the actual outflow of monies (your disbursements or expenses). You can break out the categories as needed for personal clarification. The most common ones are as follows:

Cost of goods acquired. This is the amount actually spent on the goods purchased during that period.

Sales, general, and administrative (SG&A). These costs include salaries, rent, advertising, utilities, insurance, office supplies, shipping materials, etc.

Interest Expense. This is the amount you actually paid on interest during the period.

Buildings and equipment. This is amount you pay on loans that you have taken for out for the building and equipment.

Long-term debt reduction. This is amount you pay for any loans that you may have taken out for operating capital, start-up costs, etc.

Distribution to owners. This is the amount that you might wish to give to the owners if your balance sheet looks strong and you're profitable.

Everything Fluffy had a total going out of $677,000 for 2004 and $626,000 for 2003. Note that a dividend of $15,000 was distributed to the owners in 2003 and $20,000 in 2004.

Section 3 describes the difference of funds coming in and going out, with a positive cash flow of $98,000 for 2004 and $84,000 for 2003.

Everything Fluffy had a very enviable positive cash flow both years.

Section 4 describes what happen to the cash while it remains inside the company either as cash in the checkbook or as an investment.

Everything Fluffy has kept the cash on hand for the slow months in both 2003 and 2004.

Section 5 describes the overall net change in cash position. The top half and bottom half of the cash flow statement must be the same and they are $98,000 for 2004 and $84,000 for 2003.

33. Break-even analysis

Contracting Company. A construction student wanted to start a contracting company that specialized in building $200k homes. His experience of working for other contractors indicated that he could expect to make about 10% off each home or $20k. He wanted to hire a salaried salesperson for $30k, an office manager for $25k, and a project manager for $50k. His office rent and miscellaneous expenses for the year totalled another $15k. He personally wanted to make $100k, so his "nut-to-crack" was $220k. Given those numbers, he would have to contract 11 houses ($220k÷$20k) a year to just break even–providing his company doesn't make any big mistakes.

In an earlier chapter, you learned how to perform financial snapshots. The process had you dividing what you thought the margins of a business might be into a hypothetical rent and labor expense. It was a quick and simple way of looking at the viability of a business venture. If the number was excessively high, the business probably was doomed to failure. If the number seemed reasonable, the business had a chance for success. Obviously, the weakness of the financial snapshot process was that it wasn't based on accurate data, but it was on educated guesses and hunches. Nevertheless, this is still a thought-provoking activity.

A break-even analysis is a similar process but uses more complete and accurate information. Basically, you are dividing your gross product/service margin into your total business expenses for a given period of time (i.e., a week, a month, or a year). The objective of a break-even analysis is to find out what amount of sales you'll need to generate in order to cover your business expenses. Naturally, your ultimate goal is to do much better than that in order to realize a profit. But that may take a start-up venture considerable time to accomplish. Breaking even is the first step to profitability!

Let's take a look at a simple example. Suppose we rent one of those carts that you see in the center aisles of shopping malls for a $1,000 a month to sell calendars. We hire three people to work the necessary operating hours for an additional $2,800. We have no other expenses, and those two items total out at $3,800 a month. The margin on the calendars is $10.00. Dividing $10.00 into $3,800 gives us a break-even point of 380 units. In other words, we have to sell 380 units a month to pay our expenses. Anything over 380 units will generate a profit. Anything below 380 units will generate a loss. Can it be done? It seems reasonable because you will have to sell approximately 12 calendars a day or one an hour.

Pretend that you've decided go into the teddy bear manufacturing business and that your teddy bears will wholesale for $12.00 each. When you add up the labor, thread, fabric, foam, eyes, box, and packing material, you have a production cost of $4.00. Subtracting the production cost from the selling cost gives you a gross margin of $8.00. Next you would add up all of the expenses that your business generates for a month. These would include rent, management's salary, utilities, advertising, insurance, depreciation, and similar expenses, for $16,000. Dividing $16,000 by your gross margin of $8.00 has your break even point at 2000 teddy bears a month. But if you produced and sold 2500 units, you would have a profit of $4,000 that month (500 units over break even x $8.00).

Consider a photographer who works out of his or her home and shoots only weddings. The photographer wants to earn $75,000 a year, and knows that the average wedding bills out at $2500.00. Of that $2500.00, approximately $700.00 is spent on prints, processing, and miscellaneous expenses. Hence, the photographer's margin is $1800.00. To earn $75,000, the photographer will have to shoot 42 weddings ($75,000 / $1800). That's a lot of weekends!

Two of our students–Nancy and Jane, decide to sell Christmas trees to make some spare money for a spring-break vacation. They rent a storefront for $200.00 and fabricate a sign for $100.00. They rent a truck to pick up the trees for $300.00, including gas. They buy a hundred trees for $5.00 a piece or $500.00 total. They intend to sell the trees for $25.00 each, depending on the size and quality. Their total "nut to crack" is $1100.00 or 44 trees to break even ($1100 ÷ $25.00). And that doesn't include their labor of standing in subfreezing temperatures. The good news is that once they sell 44 trees, the rest of the money is theirs to share. If they sold all the trees, they could make $1400. Unfortunately, dividing their time into that number would be heart breaking! Truth be known, they sold 72 trees total.

Restaurant story. When we were preparing our restaurant business plan, we calculated total monthly expenses at $24,000. Our food cost would be held at 25%. So we calculated that we would have to generate $30,000 a month in sales to break even. Basically we had to do a $1,000 a day in sales ($30,000/ 30 days). Based on our research of the area, customer demographics, and competition, we were confident that we could easily generate those numbers. We projected 60 lunches a day at $5.00 each for a monthly total of $9,000 and 200 nightly dinners at $8.00 each for a monthly total of $28,800. Adding the monthly lunches and dinner tabs together generated a grand total of $37,800. We were incredibly accurate in our forecasts, but didn't factor in theft.

34. Pro forma projections

Pro forma is a fancy word that refers to anything you're going to estimate. Since you are starting a business, you will want to create a pro forma income statement, balance sheet, cash flow analysis with a break-even point. These will become an important part of your business plan. The fact is, without these forecast documents you really don't have a business plan.

Putting these together is not an easy task. The success of this experience is based on educated guesses, hunches, and assumptions. The emphasis here is on educated. The more you can learn about the venture you are undertaking, the better chance your forecast has at being valid. When displaying these pro forma documents, be sure to carefully describe the parameters and assumptions that were used in generating them.

The pro forma income statement is simply designed to estimate your business revenue, expenses, and profit ahead of time. The idea here is to simply indicate how you hope your business will perform over a number of years.

The pro forma balance sheet also resembles a real historical balance sheet in layout. The difference is that you are attempting to project what you own, what you owe, and what your company will be worth over time.

The pro forma cash flow sheet also resembles a normal cash flow statement. The difference is that you are projecting where the cash will come from and how it will be used over a period of time. It is advisable to generate yearly cash flow projections until you can indicate a successful break-even point.

The pro forma break-even point is your projection of when your business will begin making a profit.

Initial money requirements 35.

The goal here is to figure out how much money you'll need to raise to get your business up and running. You basically need money for two different phases of operation: before you open for business and after you begin operation. The first-phase money would be for equipment, supplies, rent, utilities, and start-up wages. The second-phase money would be used to offset losses until you reach your break-even point, something you can predict by examining your pro forma cash flow statement.

If you've been paying attention to us, you probably have sensed that we're minimalists. We stick to the "gotta haves." We start businesses to make money, not to impress our friends with glamorous storefronts or fancy furniture. We adhere to the KISS theory–keep it simple stupid! We're bootstrappers at heart. We encourage you to do the same–at least in the beginning!

Let's start with the facility. We're going to help make this decision for you–work out of your home/apartment or rent a building/store front! We highly recommend not building or even buying your first facility. Remember–keep it simple and affordable!

Next you will need to establish the equipment required to operate your business. Our goal here is to ultimately generate a list of those unique requirements and put a dollar amount on them. A few entrepreneurs have envisioned their businesses for so long that they can tell you exactly what they need in terms of equipment and costs. But most can't. A good way to start that process is to flow chart your business. Start at the beginning of the process. What happens first? What's needed at that point? Write it down. Work your way through the various processes while simultaneously listing the various things necessary to make that happen–i.e., a desk, a phone, a chair, a computer, a display case, a fax machine. As you work your way through the flow-charting process, note what each activity is and who will perform it. That could be an easy task if you're a one-person operation, but most businesses aren't. This process can get really complicated if you're building a product with a lot of assembly steps. But forcing yourself to go through a flow charting process can uncover things you didn't think of and, sometimes, you might even discover more effective and efficient ways of accomplishing tasks.

The equipment costs you generate here belong in the **capital expenditures** category of your financial requirements because they have a useful life of over a year. We recommend that you reduce these costs by personally supplying the components you already have.

Next, you'll need to establish **start-up costs**. Start-up costs are all the expenditures involved in getting your business up and running. Obviously, if you are preparing to manufacture a product you will have design, development, prototyping, equipment preparation, personnel training, and inventory costs to anticipate. If you are offering a service, you'll have office, personnel and training costs to approximate. If you're opening a retail operation, you'll have the storefront to prepare and stock, as well as training personnel costs to include in your estimation.

Operating losses are the expenses that you will initially experience until you reach a positive cash flow. Obviously your goal is to reach a positive cash flow as quickly as possible. Some businesses do it very quickly–especially if they are dealing in cash, where the customer pays for the service or product immediately. Other businesses can take months or years to reach a positive cash flow situation. It is critical that you carefully anticipate your needs in this category. Your pro forma cash flow statements are invaluable at predicting when that might be. Even then, you are advised to add some "safety factor time frame" to allow for unanticipated events or an overestimation of sales (which is simply the biggest mistake entrepreneurs make).

Fixed costs are those expenditures that don't fluctuate with sales, like rent, basic utilities, administrative salaries, loan payments, etc.

By adding up the **capital expenditures, start-up costs, operating losses,** and **fixed costs,** you will begin to have an idea of how much money you'll need to get this business venture up and running. Oftentimes, this number is so overwhelming that many entrepreneurs just quit right here. But before you let your numbers paralyze your dream, think creatively about your real monetary needs.

Can you reduce the overall scale of your initial business idea? Will your business idea allow you to get a sizable down payment from potential customers to use for operating capital? Can you share employees with other ongoing businesses? Can you share an office, a store front, or manufacturing facilities? Can you lease equipment instead of purchasing it? Can you buy used equipment instead of new? Can you do more yourself instead of hiring others to perform tasks? (Sweat equity is a great way to reduce start-up costs.) Can you reduce the "safety-factor time frame" number, thus reducing your operating loss requirements?

Remember that where there is a will there is a way! We watched a 25 year old man raise 2.5 million to build a land-based attraction in two years. He was simply relentless at pursuing his dream.

36. Raising money

Most business ventures will simply require start-up money. If you are young (or old) and don't have any real assets, banks are really not an option for funding. Banks need something to attach for collateral, just in case you can't make loan payments. In other words, if you fail to make payments, the bank wants something to take back that they can sell to offset their losses.

If you own a home, they would be happy to loan you money against whatever amount of the house value you haven't already financed. For instance, if your house is worth $100,000 and you only financed $50,000–they would consider loaning you up to another $50,000. They would then place a second mortgage on your house, and it would become collateral for your business loan. Some entrepreneurs call this "betting the farm" on the business. Simply stated: If the business fails, you could lose your home.

So let's forget about banks for awhile. You do have a few other options that you can probe for possible business funding:

> **1. Yourself**. You could use your own savings, if you have any. That way you own it all. You get to enjoy all the profits yourself! You also assume all the risk and could lose it all as well. But that's what it's all about isn't it? Risk and gains! Just for the record, We know a number of people who have funded their dreams on credit card cash advances, which are very expensive and risky ways to pursue a business.

> **2. Family.** This is a traditional route to pursue for financing. (Gene Poor's mom has been a big investor in his dreams.) Family members could loan you the money, they could invest in your business, or they could be financially active partners. Each of those techniques comes with numerous advantages and disadvantages.

3. Friends. Like family, friends are a possible source for funding. Actually, we found that they were a valuable source of money for our business ventures. We sold stock in one our businesses, and the investors became limited partners (their financial loss obligation limited to their initial investment). We were able to raise a hundred thousand dollars very quickly by selling off 35% of the ownership in $5,000 to $10,000 amounts. Most of the investors admitted that this was a safe way for them to be involved in a start-up project without personally having to invest huge amounts of time and money and yet still be able to proudly point to the project as a minority owner–especially if it does well!

4. Angel money. Angels are wealthy people who invest in businesses with the hopes of some form of a pay-off down the road. We have a friend who started a day care center in Orlando. She was in the process of raising money by selling off shares to friends when she stumbled into a physician "angel" who was interested in financing the whole $2 million project. Many "angels" are looking for "physical things" to finance. A day care facility was perfect because it included both land and a building that the "angel" could leverage his money into. Physicians, dentists, and lawyers are classic "angel" investors. The question will always be how much ownership you are willing to give up in getting "angel" money. It is not unusual for an angel to require a majority ownership of your business venture.

5. Venture capital. Despite all the press venture capitalist get, they finance very few businesses. They literally get dozens of proposals, but very few are favorably considered. They typically are looking for high financial returns for their investment risk that very few small start-up businesses can provide. We once

83

made a favorable business presentation to a local venture capitalist group. They agreed to fund our project with the following requirements:

A. They would own 80% of the business when the money was initially loaned and progressively less ownership as the money was paid back.

B. When the money was all paid back, they would still maintain 20% ownership in the business.

C. As owners, they wanted 18% interest on the money loaned and also wanted to receive whatever profits were to be distributed at their appropriate ownership percentage.

D. They wanted a first mortgage on the building we were constructing.

E. They wanted second mortgages on both principal's personal homes.

As you can see, he or she who has the gold makes the rules. We obviously didn't take the deal.

6. Lease financing. If you are in need of business equipment, leasing is an excellent mechanism to secure that funding. The leasing company retains ownership of the equipment, and you pay a monthly fee. Often you can purchase the equipment at the end of the lease for its market value or less.

7. SBA loans. The Small Business Association will guarantee up to 90% of a loan made through banks. Start by contacting a local bank for information on how this process is established. Our experience is that this loan takes considerable time to file and to get approval. But it is a viable process to consider.

Business plan 37.

Ah, the dreaded business plan. But think about it. You wouldn't build a house without a blueprint, so why would you consider building a company without a business plan? A business plan defines your business venture and also serves as your road map to fame and fortune.

A business plan is simply a document that describes your entire business strategy, financing, competition, management, staffing, future developments, and the steps necessary to achieve your results. As you prepare it, the sheer development process forces you to think logically about where you're headed with your venture. It helps you work our details that you might not have thought about otherwise. It may even reveal new opportunities that you had not originally conceived.

More than anything, a business plan is a big reality check for you. The mere act of putting together a business plan often reveals unforeseen problems and shortcomings. Some of them can be easily addressed and repaired. However, if the problems are too big, you may decide to not move forward. Knowing when to "put-the-brakes" on a venture is never considered a negative entrepreneur quality. Actually, the ability to make an objective analysis of risk and gains is worth celebrating, especially before all the money, time, and energy go into actually creating a business that will ultimately crash and burn.

There are a number of potential audiences for your business plan. Each will look at the plan from a different vantage point. For instance, investors will seriously look at the quality, experience, and expertise of the entrepreneur, the operating management team, and the factors that will predict successful sales, growth, and profit. Bankers, on the other hand, are more interested on how fast you can repay their loan, so they'll be looking at the strength of your gross margins and cash flow

"So you want to be a good writer? Then force yourself to be a rewriter. That's where good writing happens."

Tom Sant

"Learning to write is learning to think. You don't know anything clearly unless you can state it in writing."

S.I. Hayakawa

projections. They are also looking at what assets they can use for collateral. Remember, bankers don't take risks and will probably be of no assistance in funding a start-up venture. They'll be even less useful after you're successful and don't need their help. But they'll really be there for you then!

Other audiences for your business plan include mentors, advisory board members, vendors, distributors, employees, and even customers. Be sure to think through what each of those readers might be looking for in terms of your business's viability. But when you're looking for initial start-up funding, their interests play a very minor role in the creation of a business plan.

Keep in mind that a business plan is always a work in process. It's never cast in stone. Some experts refer to it as a "living document." It is constantly being changed, improved, and updated as the business actually moves through the conception stage to execution. **Just as the journey goes from dreaming to doing!**

The tone of your writing should be conversational in nature, the same way a good storyteller unfolds a narrative. It is imperative that you be honest with yourself and your potential investors as you put your business plan together. Attempting to make the picture too bright will only cause your readers to roll their eyes. Painting a picture with too much risk might scare them away. Describing the actual advantages and disadvantages of the venture allows the potential investors to draw their own conclusions based on the information you provide.

In his book, *The Perfect Business Plan*(37), William Lasher tells us, "A good plan should be like an adventure story. It needs to excite an interested reader." In the final analysis, a business plan is a sales tool, a document used to sell your business idea. Lasher also explains that no business plan will be successful unless you tell your audience about the three "M's" of business: market, management, and money. His feeling is that other components in the business plan might be important, depending on the venture, but every plan must be strong in the three "M's."

There are dozens of templates and guidelines for business plans. But they all include basic components that will help make and defend your case for a profitable business venture. Remember, it is not the quantity of pages that will impress the reader but the substance, the quality, and the brevity. The most common business plan components include:

1. Executive summary
2. Business concept description
3. Market and industry analysis
4. The competition
5. Marketing strategy
6. Management team
7. Operations plan
8. Financial plan
9. Conclusions and appendix

Ultimately you will select components that best describe your business story. Every business plan writer will bring its unique requirements to the writing process. No two will be alike.

In the next few chapters we'll examine each of these elements in detail. Note that each segment includes a brief description of what is generally expected within that category. You'll also notice that we've also included some additional questions that you might wish to address, depending on your product or service.

38. Executive summary

An executive summary simply outlines and describes the product and service you will sell. Because it is a summary of the business plan, it is generally the last part you write based on the other information you have created and organized through-out your business plan. It really includes a positive snapshot of each of the other components that make up the business plan.

It's pretty common knowledge that not many people like to read; hence, the importance of the executive summary. Most investors will only read the executive summary–so unless you get their attention, you have a weak chance of their reading the rest of the document.

The executive summary should be absolutely no longer than 1 page–shorter if possible. It should be your best writing that will generate reader excitement and present the specifics of your idea as clearly as possible. In fairness to most investors, you have about 30 seconds to grab and hold their attention.

We have successfully raised money twice for two different businesses. In both cases the executive summary was all the investors initially saw and read. That's all they requested to see on both of our projects. Both times, the executive summary got us an opportunity to pitch the investors in person. After each of our presentations, we gave everyone a copy of our entire business plan for their review. We're big believers in the importance of a concise, exciting executive summary of your business idea–packaged professionally. See chapter 47 on business plan packaging.

Business concept description 39.

The business concept description describes your product or service in detail and explains how it specifically meets the needs of your market. Here you describe your mission (what you want your business to be) and your strategy (how you'll make it happen). Consider using descriptions of the following points:

A brief history of your idea, product, service, or business.

The precise nature and description of your business.

The positioning of your business within the industry.

The differentiation component of your business.

The mission statement of the business.

Your business model.

Your competitive advantage, strategy, and tactics.

The profit potential.

The ways technology has affected the business you're proposing.

The legal organization of your business.

Special factors that could influence your business.

The growth potential for your business.

The status of your business today and the necessary steps to move it forward

40. Market and industry analysis

The market and industry analysis section describes the market need for your product or service. This section reports the important parts of your industry and consumer research in a simple, concise, and easy-to-understand manner. Consider adding descriptions of the following points:

The overall industry–size and scope.

The attractiveness of the industry.

The state of the overall industry.

The state of the market.

The main competitors–big or small.

Any special laws and regulations.

The demographics of your business niche.

The size and geographic scope of your niche demographics.

Growth potential of your niche demographics.

Differentiation of your business within the niche.

Positioning point within the niche.

The economic trends that are favorable to your business.

The potential for expansion within your market segment.

The competition 41.

The competition section describes the direct and indirect
businesses that already service customers similar to yours. It
is very important for the reader to understand how well you
have analyzed the competitors' strengths, weaknesses, position
in the marketplace, and overall success. In this section you will
demonstrate how you will overcome the apparent competitive
obstacles and how you will succeed in the marketplace through
differentiation, untapped opportunity, and/or a unique
approach. Consider writing descriptions of the following
points:

The competitors' advantages and disadvantages

The strengths and weaknesses of the competition.

Their price/value position.

Their plans for growth and development.

Their management and employee expertise.

Their marketing efforts.

Your position within the competition arena.

Reasons why you will be successful when others haven't been.

Your differentiation and positioning advantage.

Your price/value position.

Your plans if a competitor were to adopt your advantage,
differentiation, niche, and/or strategy.

42. Marketing strategy

The marketing strategy section describes how you will get customers to buy from you. Remember, the most important success factor in any business is having customers. Without customers–nothing can happen. Explain precisely how you intend to get and keep customers. Consider writing descriptions of the following points:

Your marketing media mix.

Reasons why you'll use these mediums and what you base those decisions on–i.e., research, competition's use, focus groups, beta testing, creative hunch, etc.

Your marketing budget.

Your positioning and price point analysis as factors in your marketing plan.

Your marketing rollout and timetable.

Your use of free publicity.

The promotions you will use.

Unique marketing techniques you will use.

The people who will assist in your marketing efforts.

How you will evaluate your marketing efforts.

Management team 43.

The management team section describes why you and your team are qualified to both start and run this business. It also lists the key people, their backgrounds, and their overall responsibilities. This is a very important section because many investors consider management a key factor in overall business success. You should absolutely include the resumes of the management team. Consider writing descriptions of the following points:

Each person's important qualifications, relative experiences, and educational background.

How each of those elements will contribute to the success of the business.

The specific responsibilities of each management person.

How you will organize the management team

How this team will manage and operate the day-to-day business.

The board of directors and/or the board of advisors.

The key professional services providers, such as lawyers, bankers, and accountants.

44. Operations plan

The operations plan section describes the aspects related to providing the product and service to your specified customer base, including the facility, location, operational procedures, hours of operation, equipment requirements, special licensing arrangements, shipping, receiving, and packaging procedures. Consider writing descriptions of the following points:

A time line describing what needs to be done and when it needs to be done in order to get your business up and running.

How your business will operate on a day-to-day basis.

The availability of required talented employees.

The unique methods that your business will utilize that differentiate you from the competition.

Your quality control system.

Unique partnerships with other businesses and suppliers.

Financial plan 45.

The financial plan section describes the actual investment requirements, how the business will pay its loans back, and, ultimately, how the venture will remain viable and profitable. Ideally you should include a three-year pro forma income statement, a cash-flow statement, a balance sheet, and a break-even analysis. Consider writing descriptions of the following points:

An overview of your assumptions in generating the pro forma documents.

How long before the business reaches break-even.

How the required funds will be used.

What your contributions to the project are (e.g., money, supplies, equipment, and sweat equity).

What safety measures might be in place for difficult economic times.

Contingency plans for possible "what if" situations.

46. Conclusion and appendix

The conclusion section quickly summarizes what has been said and recommends actions for the investors to take. This is where you ask for the money! It can also be used to add additional supporting evidence to bolster some of the other sections.

The appendix section contains supplementary evidence as documentation to some of the business plan discussions. These references would include resumes, brochures, graphs, illustrations, diagrams, maps, product/facility pictures, renderings, and similar kinds of materials that might impress the investor as evidence of your research and preparation.

Presentation 47.

There are many schools of thought on how to package your final business plan. Since we are both academic visual communicators, we believe presentation is everything. A professionally prepared presentation will attract attention and ensure that you are memorable. We have witnessed literally hundreds of presentations during our careers and know the importance of packaging them creatively and professionally.

Our logic is based on the concept of face validity: you look like you can do what you say you can do. We believe what people see often will bias what they have heard or read. If there is an inconsistency, people will generally rely on what they see as evidence. So if for no other reason, why would you take a chance on a poorly presented visual package?

At the very least, the plan should be clean, well written, error free, simple, as short as possible, printed, and appropriately bound. There is a fine line between impressive and slick. You don't want to appear as if you are an extravagant, foolish spender; however, you do want to appear to be a savvy communicator who uses widely available technology.

Chances are the audience for your business plan will not be venture capitalists, but friends, relatives, and, if you're really lucky–an angel. It has been our experience that you should "step up a notch" the look of your overall presentation with that audience. For that audience, the look and feel of your business plan is almost as important as the dialogue. Quite frankly, most neophytes in the business world won't understand what your talking about and will rely mostly on your face validity and enthusiasm. We raised $100,000 from friends on a very classy looking business plan. After it was said and done, the group agreed that they were as impressed with the quality and professionalism of the visual presentation as they were with the idea.

Presentation tips.
- Use cover stock for the front and back pages.
- Use high quality white paper for the inside.
- Don't enclose the pages in plastic or laminate them.
- Use a binding method that will allow it to lie flat.
- Put a small imprint of your logo on each sheet.
- Start each section on separate sheets.
- Consider tabs for easy access to the various sections.

48. A systems approach

People often ask, "What's your favorite business model?" They are often surprised when we answer "McDonald's!" I suppose it has a lot to do with the fact that we once owned a restaurant and couldn't pull off in one place what McDonalds can do in over 28,000 sites across the world. In a word–consistency! Go anywhere in the world, and a Big Mac with fries tastes the same. We had a problem in our restaurant getting the burgers to look and taste the same between lunch and dinner.

In Michael Gerber's book *The E Myth Revisited*, he describes how Ray Kroc created much more than a giant hamburger empire; he created a model upon which an entire generation of entrepreneurs have since built fortunes through their own franchises. As Gerber explains, "The true genius of Ray Kroc's McDonald's is the Business Format Franchise."[38]

There have been franchise businesses for well over 100 years, and they are known as "trade name" franchises. A trade name franchise allows the franchisor the right to sell a nationally known product. Ford and Coca-Cola are examples of a trade name franchise. But Ray Kroc went one step further in that he provided not only the name but an **entire system** of doing business. He provided a model or "Franchise Prototype."

Gerber also explains that the, "Business Format Franchise is built on the belief that the true product of a business is not what it sells but how it sells it. The true product of a business is the business itself." Thus the name "Turn-Key Operation." The franchisor merely turns the key to success!

What Ray Kroc really did was create a foolproof business. A business that would work no matter who bought it, where they put it, and who they hired to work in it. Gerber refers to this as "A systems-dependent business, not a people-dependent business." It is, in essence, a "systems approach" to doing

98

business, and Ray Kroc introduced that concept to the entrepreneur's world.

Every entrepreneur who starts up a business can learn from Ray Kroc's system even if he or she never have more than one location. In other words, a systems approach identifies exactly how every detail of an operation needs to be performed and then trains the staff to execute it precisely as the entrepreneur determined that it should be. Nothing should be left to chance. Nothing should be undefined. Every detail is specified in the prototype or model–it is a set of standard operating procedures.

For you, as a new entrepreneur, a systems approach is a powerful concept to incorporate into your business from the very onset of the venture. If you don't do it from the beginning, you will do it somewhere along the way out of survival desperation and then, unfortunately, you will always be playing "catch-up."

In order to begin incorporating a systems approach to a start-up business, Gerber suggests the following six rules:
1. Your model should provide consistent value to all involved beyond what they generally expect.
2. Your model will be operated by people with the minimum level of skill needed.
3. Your model will be a standard of order and excellence.
4. Your specific work in the model will be described in a procedure and operations manual.
5. Your model will provide a consistent and predictable service to the customer.
6. Your model will include a specific dress and facilities code.[39]

Start now developing your business's systems approach or forever be playing quality and service catch-up!

49. Professional help

After you settle into operating your business, you'll begin looking for new ideas, technologies, and ways to solve problems. And in many cases, you won't have anyone to turn to for help. That's when you'll fully understand how important conferences, associations, trade shows, seminars, workshops, and even trade magazines can be for your continued professional development.

There is a wealth of information available for you out there– if and when you decide to participate. There are local, state, national, and international meetings to choose from–many of which have their own trade shows, conferences, and workshops. And no matter what field your business is in, there is at least one magazine dealing with that subject matter. You probably won't be able to find it on the local magazine rack. Typically specialized magazines are connected with the appropriate associations. Check on line!

For instance, we're interested in theme-park development. Currently, there are six major magazines that specialize in that arena: *Park World*, *Entertainment Management*, *InterPark*, *Attractions Management*, and *Behind the Themes*. There are also two major organizations: the International Association of Amusement Parks and Attractions (IAAPA) and the Themed Entertainment Association (TEA). There are also a number of minor organizations that serve the European and Asian markets.

Bootstrapping 50.

A Poor story. When Gene Poor designed and built a restaurant back in the late 80's, he basically created what was called a "fern bar" on the West Coast. It included lots of wood, brass, leaded glass, belt-driven fans, novel antiques, and live plants (hence the "fern" term). It was and (still is) a very eloquent Victorian statement–where too much was not enough.

After he had been in the restaurant business for a few years, a close friend came to town who had originally watched him sweat and strain to put his elaborate restaurant project together. But on this visit, Gene decided to take his friend to a new, "booming" restaurant in a nearby town. The story of that restaurant follows: A husband and wife owned a hardware store together, and one day the wife announced that she wanted to open a restaurant. The husband said, "Fine" and pushed some shelves and racks over to the side. He pointed to the vacant space and said, "Put your table and chairs here, and your kitchen over there." And that's exactly what she did and named the place Grumpies–after her endearing husband.

So when Poor and his friend entered Grumpies, the place was indeed packed with eager customers. As the two walked through the front door, Poor's friend turned and said, "You know Poor, you try too hard!"

Grumpies restaurant is the best example of bootstrapping we can think of. Bootstrapping is simply the bare-bone testing and financing of a business concept.

Now after 25 years and several physical moves, Grumpies is a great, stand-alone restaurant that is still booming. But the original concept was "beta tested" within a hardware store atmosphere. The notion was that if the wife's restaurant idea could make it in that hardware environment, it could make it anywhere.

51. Reverse engineering

We personally believe that reverse engineering is one of the most powerful ways an entrepreneur can learn about business. We're sure that academic institutions are afraid of discussing it because of the plagiarism implications. They have traditionally drilled into students that everyone should do their own work– all of their own work. Reverse engineering, at first inspection, smacks of copying or stealing someone else's idea. But that's not the case at all. When examined closely and applied correctly, it is a legitimate way to establish what is going on in a specific field or within a particular individual's skill level.

We're also convinced that most sport professionals use the reverse engineering technique all the time. For instance, we're sure that Tiger Woods reverse engineered his golf hero's swings when he was a kid, and he probably still does. We are also sure that famous musicians, artists, designers, and inventors have all reverse engineered their hero's work. (Tom Edison openly admitted it.) Reverse engineering allowed them to study and establish what another professional's benchmark of skill excellence were all about. Did they emulate that excellence? Maybe at first. But eventually they probably improved upon it and refined it. Ultimately, they made it personal by developing their own unique style.

Reverse engineering is defined as a process of extracting know-how or knowledge from a human-made artifact, business model, or skill. It has a long history of being an acceptable practice in manufacturing, and it is used in almost all professions to some degree and fashion.

Let's take a look at what two attorneys, Pamela Samuelson and Suzanne Scotchmer, have to say about reverse engineering in their paper, *The Law and Economics of Reverse Engineering*.[40] "Reverse engineering is fundamentally directed to discovery and learning. Engineers learn the state of art not just by reading printed publications, going to technical conferences, and working on projects for their firms, but also by reverse engineering others' products. Learning what has been done before often leads to new products and advances in know-how. Reverse engineering may be a slower and more expensive way for information to percolate through a technical community than patenting or publication, but it is nonetheless an effective source of information. Of necessity, reverse engineering is a form of dependent creation, but this does not taint it, for in truth all innovators stand on the shoulders of both giants and midgets. Progress in science and the useful arts is advanced by dissemination of know-how, whether by publication, patenting, or reverse engineering."

A lot of great ideas come from reverse engineering things that aren't related to a problem you're working on. Mathematician John von Neumann reverse engineered poker table behavior and developed the "game theory" model of economics. Henry Ford got his assembly line idea for manufacturing cars from watching meat packers break the process down into individual tasks. Even Gutenberg got his printing press idea from a wine press. Wild ideas can come from anywhere, and the wider you search, the better chance you'll have of making unusual connections work for you.

We recommend creating a "swipe file" (or if you feel more comfortable, an "inspiration file") to keep good ideas that others have used successfully. We have a separate one for brochures, video, web sites, exhibits, photography, businesses, and even one for great writing. (Where do you think all these quotes came from?) We often visit them just for a good dose of inspiration.

"To be really creative, you need a wide bandwidth of interests."
Randy Root

"Knute Rockne got the idea for his famous four horseman backfield shift while watching a burlesque chorus routine. Dan Bricklin took the spreadsheet concept from accounting and turned it into VisiCalc."
Roger von Oech

"Swipe from the best, then adapt."
Tom Peters

"Creativity is defined as seeing something in something else."
Saul Bass

In the film *Hale, Hale Rock-n-Roll*, Eric Clapton describes how Chuck Barry wrote the rules for playing rock-n-roll on the guitar. Chuck Barry then goes on to describe how he reverse engineered other guitar players rifts and combined them into his style.

52. Intrapreneuring

As we stated at the beginning of our journey, the term entrepreneur has taken on a broader definition. It's now defined as a state of mind. It's about having a passion for doing something an individual loves. It's about an individual's spirit. It's about a "can-do" attitude. It's about an individual's unique, opportunity-seeking mind-set. This "new entrepreneur" is one who likes to do things differently. He or she likes to bend the rules and excite the world with off-the-wall ideas. The "new entrepreneur" is typically looking for unique opportunities in which to direct his or her passion and energy. The "new entrepreneur" is about creativity, innovation, ideas, and change.

And all of that can be said about an intrapreneur as well, except he or she applies those characteristics within an existing business organization. Of the dozens of people we know who manifest intrapreneurial characteristics, the one who immediately comes to mind is Shane McCall. Shane is the Senior Manager of Visual Merchandising for American Girl Place. Shane's passion for visual merchandising is contagious. He is constantly thinking about new projects within the store environment. By always looking for new ideas, his notion is that "you have to be creative in researching new ways in being creative." You can instantly get a sense of Shane's intrapreneurial spirit by walking through an American Girl store in Chicago or New York City. The stores are absolutely stunning.

Interestingly enough, Shane works within a store concept that was originally started in 1985 by an entrepreneur named Pleasant Rowland. She created the American Girl brand as a way to educate and entertain girls with quality books, dolls, and toys that integrate learning and play experiences while emphasizing important traditional values. Mattel acquired the American Girl business in 1998 and continues to operate it as a separate subsidiary in Middleton, Wisconsin.[41]

Bid it out! 53.

It is so easy for entrepreneurs to get caught up with the day-to-day minutia that they don't seek bids from their suppliers. Seeking low bids is a simple procedure that will drastically reduce a businesses cash "burn rate" and ultimate profitability. It doesn't have to be done every week, but twice a year keeps your vendors honest and on their toes. Remember, they're also running a business and constantly adjusting their prices to achieve a strong bottom line.

Let us give a prime example of an industry that affects almost every business–printing. The printing industry is a classic "niche" industry. The very nature of printing is that it relies on expensive equipment and experiences rapid shifts in technology. It has to "niche" to survive. Few can afford to be all things to all people. So it behooves entrepreneurs to seek out the printer who works within the format niche they're seeking (i.e., business cards, brochures, newsletters, envelopes, letterheads, etc.)

Before we knew about niche printers, we were seeking a printer for a 100-page, full-color, perfect-bound textbook. We bid the project out to three local printers, but it wasn't really their specialty. When we received the bids, they ranged from $24,000 to $36,000 for 500 copies. By chance (before we selected one of the bids) we found a book similar to what we were having printed and found the printer's name on the credits page. We called and had that printer bid our project. It was their niche, and they bid the job at $12,500. We saved at least $12,000 by using the right printer for the job, even though the printer was three states away.

The moral of the story, "Keep your suppliers on their toes–bid it out."

54. Franchises

If you still believe you have the entrepreneurial spirit but the challenge of developing a brand new business is just too overwhelming, you might want to consider buying a franchise. Basically a franchise is a license to operate a branch of an existing business with an established brand name. The franchisee (you) pay an initial fee and ongoing royalties to the franchisor (them). For these payments, the franchisor grants the use of their trademark, provides ongoing support and training, allows the use of their unique systems of doing business, and confers the right to sell their product or provide their service.

The primary reason of buying a franchise, rather than starting from scratch, is that the failure rate among franchised business is much lower. Basically the franchisee is benefitting from the past experience of the franchisor who has identified an effective and profitable business model that may have been duplicated hundreds or thousands of times. In the *Franchise Opportunities Handbook*,[42] LaVerne Ludden describes a number of other franchise advantages including:
- National advertising campaigns.
- Incredible group buying power.
- Training and support systems.
- Site selection services and start-up assistance.

Ludden also explains that there are some serious drawbacks to entering into a franchise, including:
- Franchise fees and royalties can be crippling.
- Enforced product or service standardizations.
- Market saturation for product or service.

In summary, franchising offers an entrepreneur an acceptable way to enter into a business venture. But you must be as methodical with your research as you would be in terms of starting a conventional business. Buyer beware! Being a franchisee is like a marriage–you two must be compatible.

Final thoughts 55.

Most of our entrepreneurial experiences involved providing customers with high-ticket, customized services or products. These specialized experiences are often very difficult to deliver because you're dealing with two things that people value the most–their dreams and their money. Some of those experiences have become immutable laws of operation for us. Consider these as you move forward with your venture:

- Never second-guess anyone's ability to buy.
- Never sign a contract with a penalty clause.
- Never guarantee a job with personal assets.
- Treat every job as it was the most important one you've ever done.
- Under-promise and over-deliver.
- Plan on the fact that everything will take longer then planned.
- Never give anything away–it has no value to the recipient.
- Get sign-offs on all important issues.
- Try to get everything in writing.
- Attempt to prepare bullet-proof contract proposals–as they are the first key to overall project success.
- Identify and utilize a strong project manager.
- Identify one key person within the client team for all sign-offs and approvals.
- Establish a standard turn-around time for all approvals.
- Establish a limit on approval loops–if at all possible.
- Clearly state how approval-loop delays will effect the ultimate project due date.
- Be sure that your payment schedule is front-end loaded or at least keep payments in balance with the production schedule.
- If it starts out dumb–it will only get dumber.
- Savior the journey and enjoy the ride.

56. Notes

1. Michael Ray and Rochelle Myers, *Creativity in Business* (New York: Doubleday, 1989), 3.

2. Guy Kawasaki, *The Art of the Start* (New York: Penguin Group, 2004), xi.

3. Ibid, 4-5.

4. World Business, "Entrepreneurs Under the Spotlight," cnn.com, February 3, 2005.

5. Jeffrey Fox, *How to Make Big Money in Your Own Business* (New York: Hyperion Books, 2004), 22-23.

6. Roger von Oech, *A Kick in the Seat of the Pants* (New York: Harper and Row, 1986), 14-15.

7. Charles Thompson, *What a Great Idea!* (New York: Harper-Collins, 1992), 9-22.

8. Peter Drucker, *The Daily Drucker* (NewYork: HarperCollins, 2004), 80.

9. Harvard Business Essentials, *Entrepreneur's Toolkit* (Boston: Harvard Business School Publishing, 2005), 14.

10. Kim Gordon, "3 Rules for Niche Marketing," Entrepreneur.com, March 04, 2002.

11. Jungle Jim's Market, "The Story of Jim Bonaminio," junglejims.com, February 27, 2005.

12. Watts Wacker and Jim Taylor, *The Visionary's Handbook* (New York: HarperCollins, 2000), 39-55.

13. Roy Williams, *The Wizard of Ads* (Austin Texas: Bard Press, 1998), 98.

14. Guy Kawasaki, *The Art of the Start* (New York: Penguin Group, 2004), 30.

15. John Maxwell, *Thinking For A Change* (New York: Time Warner, 2003), 207-222.

16. Jack Canfield, *The Success Principles* (New York: Harper-Collins, 2005), 306-313.

17. Stephen Heiman and Diane Sanchez, *The New Strategic Selling* (New York: Warner Books, 1998), 46.

18. Michel Robert, *Strategy Plain and Simple II* (New York: McGraw Hill, 1998), xi-xiv.

19. Ibid, 1-16.

20. "Holiday World Pop Update," *Funworld Magazine*, February 2005, pg. 7.

21. Michel Robert, *Strategy Plain and Simple II* (New York: McGraw Hill, 1998), 77-87.

22. Jim Collins, *Good to Great* (New York: Harper Collins, 2001), 95.

23. Harvard Business Essentials, *Entrepreneur's Toolkit* (Boston, Massachusetts: Harvard Business School Publishing, 2005), 46.

24. Duncan Brock (ed.), *The Lexus Story* (New York: Melcher Media, 2003), 61.

25. Jeffrey Abrahams, *The Mission Statement Book* (Berkely, Ca: Ten Speed Press, 1999), 8.

26. Ibid, 14.

27. Eric Shultz, *The Marketing Game* (Holbrook, Ma: Adams Media, 1999), 8-9.

28. Jim Wegryn, "An Old Lady and a Mop," imwegryn.com/ Names/Commercial, February 2, 2005.

29. Rieva Lesonsky, *Start Your Own Business* (Irvine, Ca: Entrepreneur Media, 2004), 490-493.

30. Amanda Ruth and Allen Wysocki, "Top Sellers: Characteristics of a Top Salesperson," edis.ifas.ufl.edu/pdffiles

31. Robert Kreitner, *Management* (New York: Houghton Mifflin, 1998), 5.

32. Learning - Leadership Development Committee, Synod of Alberta and the Territories, albertasynod.ca/resources/leadership/think_abouts/good_managers.

33. Tom Peters, *Re-imagine* (New York: Dorling Kindersley, 2003), 320.

34. Eric Shultz, *The Marketing Game* (Holbrook, Ma: Adams Media, 1999), 84.

35. Roy Williams, *The Wizard of Ads* (Austin, Tx: Bard Press, 1998), 70-71.

36. Tom Kelley, *The Art of Innovation,* (New York: Doubleday, 2001), 81-83.

37. William Lasher, *The Perfect Business Plan* (New York: Doubleday, 1994), 3.

38. Michael Gerber, *The E Myth Revisited* (New York: Harper-Collins, 2001), 79-96.

39. Ibid, 97-113.

40. Pamela Samuelson and Suzanne Scotchmer, "The Law and Economics of Reverse Engineering," sims.berkeley.edu/~pam/papers, December 3, 2001.

41. American Girl Place, "The Story of American Girl" Americangirl.com, February 12, 2005.

42. LaVerne Ludden, *Franchise Opportunities Handbook* (Indianapolis, Ind: Jist Works, 1999), 22-26.

Amortized. A method of distributing the cost of an investment over the quantity manufactured or sold.

Assets. Anything of value owned by the business, such as cash, accounts receivable, equipment, facility, and property.

Big ticket. Products or services that are very expensive.

Bootstrapping. Using creative and frugal techniques to finance the start-up phase of a business venture.

Bottom feeder. A company that competes with the lowest possible price and generally the worst quality.

Break-even. The point at which your total sales margins equal your total costs. (Sales after break-even contribute to profit.)

Burn rate. The rate at which a start-up uses capital provided by investors until it becomes profitable.

Business model. Describes the way a business venture proposes to make money.

Business model innovation. A unique component that revolutionizes how products or services are sold in an industry.

Business to business (B2B). A company that sells primarily to another business.

Bulletproof. An impeccable document, service, or product.

Cash flow. The amount of cash a company takes in minus the amount it pays out.

Co-branding. A relationship between two or more companies in which they promote each other's products or services.

Core competency. A company's unique skill or quality that serves as a competitive advantage over its competition.

Cross-selling. Recommending or referring to another company's product or service.

111

Demographics. A set of characteristics that describes a particular group of people.

Distribution channel. The route a product takes from manufacturing to the its final customer.

Doing Business As (DBA). When sole proprietors do business under a different name than their own, they are required to submit appropriate DBA forms to the county clerk's office.

Elevator speech. A brief verbal statement that demonstrates the merits of a particular company.

Emerging industry. A new venture in which standard operating procedures have not been developed.

Equity. The owners interest in a business (minus any loans).

Employee Stock Ownership Plans (ESOP). Various methods of transferring ownership of a company to its employees.

Exit strategy. A plan that describes how the owners will sell their interest in the company.

Face validity. The ability to look like you can do what you say you can do in person or in a document.

Factoring. A very expensive process of selling accounts receivable to another company at a discount rate and receiving the money up-front to improve cash flow.

Fixed expenses. Business expenses that do not change each month, for example, rent, equipment leases, and salaries.

Float. The time period given to a customer to pay a bill.

Focus groups. Small groups of people who resemble potential clients who are used to determine a product or service viability.

Fragmented industry. An industry characterized by a large number of equal competitors (in size and service).

Gazelles. Fast-growth companies or hot-shot new employees.

Gross profit. The amount of money left after you pay the cost of sales.

Honeymoon. A period of time that sales are great because the business is new and people are eager to just try it.

Industrial espionage. The practice of collecting information about a competitor through devious methods.

Initial Public Offering (IPO). The first sale of a company's stock to the public.

Intellectual property. The essential idea about a new product or service that makes the development possible. Typically, it can be protected through a legal means such as a patent or copyright.

Liabilities. The amount of money a company owes.

Life cycle. The four stages of a product/service life: embryonic, growth, mature, and decline.

Line of credit. A pre-established bank loan of a set amount that you can draw from as needed.

Liquidity. The ability to convert an asset into cash.

Mature industry. An industry that shows little or no growth potential.

Merger. The combining of two or more companies into one.

Milestone. An important event in the development of business.

Net income. Money left over after all company expenses have been paid (also called net profit).

Net worth. The total company's worth minus what it owes.

Non-compete clause. An agreement that employees (and sometimes suppliers) sign indicating that they won't steal your idea and either go work for someone else or start their own company. Usually it is for a set time period of time.

Non-disclosure agreement. A legal document in which a person agrees not to divulge private information.

Nut to crack. Break-even point.

Outsourcing. The use of outside consultants, free lancers, and companies to provide certain services such as advertising or training.

Psychographics. A relatively new marketing term that refers to a customer's values and attitudes toward a product/service.

Rainmaker. A person who sells.

Return on investment (ROI). The amount of money you get back after you make an investment in something (e.g., a piece of machinery, an advertising campaign, a new product line)

Seed money. The initial investment made in a business venture.

Sign-off. A point where a client approves in writing what has been done so far.

Start-up costs. The amount of money needed to get the business up and running.

Sunk costs. Money spent that the business can never recover.

Tag line. A catch phrase that is typically used with a logo in literature.

Through-put. Describes the number of people who can receive a service or product in a particular time frame.

Venture capital. Money provided to start-ups by private investors for a percentage of stock and profits.

Window of opportunity. The best time period for a company to enter the marketplace.

Working capital. Cash on hand to pay expenses.